MW00653842

Cover art:
   Antoniazzo Romano (c. 1430–1508/12), *Madonna and Child.*

THE
VIRTUES OF MARY

THE
VIRTUES OF MARY

WITH A SHORT DISSERTATION ON THE
SALVE REGINA

BY

L. LANZONI

*Provost General
Of the Institute of Charity*

Ave, gratia plena (Lk 1: 28)

Academy of the Immaculate
New Bedford, MA
2012

The Virtues of Mary, is a book prepared for publication by the Franciscans of the Immaculate [marymediatrix.com], POB 3003, New Bedford, MA, 02741-3003.

© Franciscans of the Immaculate 2012
All rights reserved

Originally printed:

LONDON

R. & T. WASHBOURNE, 4 PATERNOSTER ROW, E.C.
BENZINGER BROTHERS, NEW YORK
1903

Imprimatur.

HERBERTUS CARDINALIS VAUGHN,

Archiepiscopus Westmonasteriensis

Cum Permissu Superiorum

ISBN: 978-1-60114-057-9

CONTENTS

―――――

PART I.

The Virtues of Mary in relation to God.

PART II.

The Virtues of Mary in relation to Men.

PART I I I.

The Virtues of Mary in relation to Herself.

LIST OF ILLUSTRATIONS

These images are from the works of Joseph Sebastian Klauber (1700–1768). They can be found at *http://campus.udayton.edu/mary/prayers/litanylor.html* along with an explanation of each title and other titles of the Blessed Virgin Mary in the Litany of Loretto.

Permission to reprint these images has been received from *The Mary Page* at: *www.udayton.edu/mary/* of The Marian Library/International Marian Research Institute, University of Dayton, Dayton, Ohio (USA).

Adeamus - ad thronum gratiæ. Hebr. 4.

INTRODUCTION

This very clear and inspiring study of the virtues of Our Lady by Fr. Luigi Lanzoni, Provost General of the Institute of Charity, otherwise known as the Rosminians, first appeared in Italian in 1895. Shortly thereafter an English version, prepared by Fr. Edward Hoare of the same Institute, was jointly published in 1903 by R. & T. Washbourne of London and Benziger Brothers of New York. At the time of its publication the learned author of this work, a highly esteemed priest, was one of the best interpreters of Bl. Antonio Rosmini-Serbati (1797–1855), Founder of the Institute of Charity and perhaps the greatest of 19th century Italian Catholic philosophers. Fr. Lanzoni also was a theologian-philosopher in his own right, and no minor director of souls. Today, both Fr. Lanzoni and his wonderful meditations on the virtues of Our Lady are so forgotten as to seem never to have existed, yet they deserve better.

Fr. Lanzoni was born on April 24, 1836, in Mantua, Italy. His family was very prosperous, but more so Catholic. Endowed with an excellent mind and beneficiary of good religious and intellectual formation both at home under his mother's direction, and then in school, he progressed rapidly in his studies. As an adolescent he was already acquainted with the writings of Bl. Antonio Rosmini; and in 1856, shortly after beginning the study of theology in Rome, he entered the Institute of Charity. There, he enjoyed as his teachers, some of the Founder's great collaborators. In 1859, he was ordained priest. Thereafter he continued his studies, and labored with great success as teacher, master of novices and spiritual director in university circles. In 1877, he was chosen Provost General and continued in this office until his death on January 5, 1901. During his years as superior general, controversy over the orthodoxy of the writings of Rosmini, which had begun during the lifetime of the Blessed, reached its bitter climax with the condemnation of numerous propositions, false in themselves, said to be present in these works and with the listing of many of Rosmini's works in the Index of Forbidden Books. The saintly prudence and heroic obedience of Fr. Lanzoni contributed in no small way to both the salvation of his Order and the works of Rosmini. With their recommendation to Catholic students of philosophy and theology in the Encyclical *Fides et Ratio* of Pope John Paul II, and the removal of his works from the Index of Forbidden Books, it is clear that while the condemned propositions are indeed false, they are not found in the works of Rosmini. This also happens to have been the position of Bl. Pius IX when the controversy first began during the lifetime of Bl. Antonio.

Fr. Lanzoni was not only a spiritual disciple of Bl. Antonio, but an intellectual one as well, as the list of his editions of the major works of Rosmini and his own published works abundantly demonstrate. This, among other reasons, is what makes his work on the virtues of Mary so important, not only for theologians but for believers in general as well. Rosmini was called to heaven in 1855 before he had time to complete his major, projected work on salvation history, the sixth book of which was to be a treatise on the role of the Virgin Mary in the plan of salvation. The Blessed died before he had begun work on the last two books of this *opus*. That it would have treated the virtues of Mary is beyond question and that the meditations of Fr. Lanzoni reflect Marian convictions of Bl. Antonio is perfectly evident from the central focus of the meditations: charity, the characteristic feature of the Institute of Charity. While the considerations offered for reflection are clear and moving, they are also rich in theological and philosophical insight so characteristic of those who, like Bl. John Duns Scotus, stress what is known in theology as the "primacy of charity." And it is a fact that, in much of his philosophical work, Rosmini was not only influenced by St. Thomas, but by Bl. John Duns Scotus as well.

To fully appreciate this depth, it is necessary to place Fr. Lanzoni's work in the Church's ancient and on-going tradition of imitating the virtues of Mary. Today, this practice is popularly associated with consecration to the Immaculate Heart as taught in the messages of Our Lady at Fatima and confirmed by Our Lord himself as representing His will; but we are no longer very familiar with the antecedents of this tradition. Over the past century or so, we have become accustomed to biographies of Our Lady which approximate, as much as possible, the hagiographical bias of our times: to stress what Mary has in common with the ordinary person rather than what makes her unique as a person: her all-holiness, her all-blessedness; in a word, the reason why she defined herself at Lourdes as the Immaculate Conception. This is exactly the point of reference for the ancient biographies of Mary: to illustrate her virtues, above all. For, by reason of her all-holiness, by reason of her title as Panhaghia-Beatissima these virtues reveal her person and personality, what it means to be the *Speculum justitiae*: Mirror of Justice, the perfect reflection of Jesus who is the Sun of Justice. When we imitate Mary's virtues, we become like her as a holy person. A Saint very much of our times, Maximilian M. Kolbe, put it this way: we are transubstantiated into her person and so into the Holy Spirit, of whom she is the Spouse.

But perhaps of all the saints, St. Francis of Assisi is the one who has given classic expression to this fundamental principle of Christian piety, prayer and holiness: the imitation of Mary's virtues or consecration to the Immaculate Heart. For him, Lady Poverty, the virtue so characteristic of the Order he founded is, literally, Our Lady. When

Francis addresses Lady Poverty, he is, in fact, addressing the Mother of God. He gives more concrete expression to this principle in his *Salutation of the Blessed Virgin* and *Salutation of the Virtues*, two apparently distinct works, yet inseparable; and not merely inseparable, but interchangeable. They show expressly how both the Church and the single members of the Church, to the degree they are holy, are extensions of Mary's virtue and her work as Mediatrix of all grace in the souls of believers and potential believers. Here are the two salutations:

Salutation of the Blessed Virgin

Hail, O Lady,
Holy Queen,
Mary, holy Mother of God;
You are the Virgin made Church
And the one chosen by the most holy Father in
heaven
whom He consecrated with His most holy
beloved Son
and with the Holy Spirit the Paraclete,
in whom there was and is all the fullness of
grace and every good.
Hail, His Palace!
Hail, His Tabernacle!

Hail, His Home!
Hail, His Robe!
Hail, His Servant!
Hail, His Mother!
And [hail] all you holy virtues
> *which through the grace and light of the Holy*
> > *Spirit*
> *are poured into the hearts of the faithful*
> *so that from their faithless state*
> *you may make them faithful to God.*

Mary is the fullness of grace because her entire person, consecrated by the Father with the Son and Holy Spirit, is the incorporation of all virtue in her person, the very reason she is Mediatrix of all grace to bring the faithful from a state of faithlessness or vice to one of fidelity to God, or virtue. In his Rule (chapter nine), this is what St. Francis commands his friars to preach, above all, by good example: virtue and vice, punishment and glory. When this is done concretely, this is to preach the glory of Mary, Mother of God and of all good, and our Mother.

Salutation of the Virtues

Hail, Queen Wisdom, may the Lord protect you
> *with your sister, holy pure Simplicity.*
Lady, holy Poverty, may the Lord protect you
> *with your sister, holy Humility.*

Lady, holy Charity, may the Lord protect you
*   with your sister, holy Obedience.*
O most holy Virtues, may the Lord protect all of you,
*   from Whom you come and proceed.*
There is surely no one in the entire world
*   who can possess any one of you*
*   unless he dies first.*
Whoever possesses one [of you]
*   and does not offend the others,*
*   possesses all.*
And whoever offends one [of you],
*   does not possess any,*
*   and offends all.*

And each one destroys vices and sins.

Holy Wisdom destroys
*   Satan and all his subtlety.*
Pure holy Simplicity destroys
*   all the wisdom of this world*
*   and the wisdom of the body.*
Holy Poverty destroys
*   the desire of riches*
*   and avarice*
*   and the riches of this world.*
Holy Humility destroys
*   pride*
*   and all the people who are in the world*
*   and all things that belong to the world.*
Holy Charity destroys
*   every temptation of the devil and of the flesh*
*   and every carnal fear.*

Holy Obedience destroys
   every wish of the body and of the flesh
   and binds its mortified body
   to obedience of the Spirit
   and to obedience of one's brother.
And [the person who possesses her] is subject and
    submissive
   to all persons in the world
   and not only to man only
   but even to all beasts and wild animals
   so that they may do whatever they want with him
   inasmuch as it has been given to them from
    above by the Lord.

Perfect virtue, then, is Our Lady, and each of the particular virtues an aspect of her holy personality. Perfect virtue does to vice exactly what the Immaculate Virgin does to the head of the Serpent: crushes it. And if anyone wishes to know her person more precisely, he need only meditate on how she practiced the virtues. Scripture and Tradition, as Fr. Lanzoni notes, offer us abundant material to understand this great truth. Hence, it is not too difficult to understand why, after the time of St. Francis, not only were the virtues of Mary cultivated in the lives of the faithful, but a great devotion to the virtues of Mary arose—sometimes presented in the manner of St. Francis as six; other times delineated in a sequence of ten as by St. Jeanne; and at times, explained by Fr. Lanzoni as expressions of the perfect exercise of charity: love of God and love of neighbor as oneself, just as Mary, under the Cross, lived prayer and penance in union with her Son and Savior, Jesus.

Here are two examples of this devotion illustrating how the imitation of Mary's virtues is the foundation of what Our Lady calls prayer and penance or perfect conformity to Christ crucified.

In the late fifteenth century St. Jeanne de Valois, daughter of King Louis XI and wife of King Louis XII of France, after having been repudiated by the latter as wife and queen of France—in 1501, together with her spiritual director, the Franciscan Bl. Gilbert Nicolas, founded the Order of the Annunciades, or the Sisters of the Annunciation of the Blessed Virgin Mary. This was an order of penance and prayer, whose rule, composed by Bl. Gilbert, primarily consisted in imitating the ten virtues of Mary as shown in the Gospels. St. Jeanne composed the chaplet of the ten virtues to be prayed in honor of the Virgin; and she herself had resolved to imitate the Blessed Virgin, especially in the practice of silence and humility. The ten virtues in this rule are descriptions of Mary as most pure, prudent, humble, faithful, devout, obedient, poor, patient, merciful, and sorrowful. These ten, in one way or another, are found in the six of St. Francis. Without doubt, a rule of life based on the imitation of Mary's virtues had not a little to do with strengthening the Church in France to resist the Protestant denial of the importance of "good works" for salvation.

A later example is that of the Marians of the Immaculate Conception [founded during the seventeenth century in Poland] whose rule also centered about the imitation of the ten virtues of Mary, symbolized by a star with ten rays to be worn on the habits of the religious, and praying the chaplet of the ten virtues, which of old, hung from the sash of their white habits. Imitation of the virtues of Mary is in fact the prayer best suited to honor the Mother of God.

I cite the example of the Marians of the Immaculate Conception because the association of the imitation of the virtues of Mary with the mystery of the Immaculate Conception, or consecration to the Immaculate Heart, pinpoints the core of this exercise of prayer, devotion and penance as a form of life based on the mystery of the Immaculate Conception. All virtue, when perfectly exercised, is an expression of this mystery and of what it means to be a perfect person in the image and likeness of the one and triune God. This is exactly what St. Francis had in mind in his salutes to the Virgin and to the Virtues.

If we compare the listing of St. Francis: six virtues of Our Lady; and that of St. Jeanne and the Marians: ten virtues; with that of Fr. Lanzoni, based on the essence of holiness: the observance of love of God and of neighbor as oneself, we can immediately perceive his fidelity to tradition and original insights.

In conclusion, a word of thanks to the superiors of the Institute of Charity who so graciously gave their permission to the Academy of the Immaculate to reprint the English version of this precious work (already republished in Italian in somewhat abridged form in 1995).

We also take this occasion to salute the

genial translator of this work, Fr. Edward Hoare of the Institute of Charity, and a personal disciple of Fr. Lanzoni. Fr. Hoare was born in Brisbane, Australia, in 1863. As a young man he converted from Anglicanism to the Catholic Church, joined the Rosminians, was ordained priest and labored extensively and fruitfully for the sanctification of souls in England. He died in 1929 in Loughborough (England), much respected and beloved of all. We think his translator's note dated Rugby, 1903, a fitting conclusion to this introduction.

> This little book was translated from the Italian and printed for private circulation in 1897. It is now offered to the public in the hope that it may contribute to promote a tender devotion to the Mother of Jesus.

Fr. Peter M. Fehlner, F.I.

AUTHOR'S PREFACE

———

Though we adore God alone and render to Him alone the honour and glory that are due from the creature to the Creator,[1] nevertheless, as part of our worship of God we honour and invoke the friends most dear to Him, namely, His angels and saints, and we offer them our tribute of loving service and devotion.

Now since God's own Mother is beyond all measure dearer to Him than His friends can be, therefore we venerate Mary, the Mother of God, with a special honour far higher than that which we give to angels and saints. It is the loving, filial reverence with which Jesus Christ first honoured her during His life on earth,[2] and which Christians have continued to yield her with love increasing from age to age, as Mary herself foresaw and predicted. "Behold, from henceforth all generations shall call me blessed."[3] Hence it is that every year has its

———

[1] 1 Tim 1: 17.

[2] Lk 2: 51.

[3] Lk 1: 48.

Month of Mary, every month has its festivals in her honour, every week has Saturday dedicated to her and finally every day invites us by the sound of the *Angelus-bell,* morning, noon, and evening to pay our homage to Mary. Every year, and month, and week, and day, Christian hearts feel the need of honouring and invoking their merciful, kind, sweet mother, who is the Mother of God. They know well that the honour given to the Mother of God terminates in her divine Son, even as the worship of the Son redounds to the glory of the Mother. "Assuredly, all that we say in praise of the Mother pertains to the Son, and again, when we honour the Son we cease not to glorify the Mother."[1]

It was to nourish this filial devotion towards Mary that so many books have been written, more perhaps than have been composed on any other spiritual subject. With this same intent I have written this little book on the Virtues of Mary, in the hope that you may gain as much fruit from reading it as I did from writing it.

L. LANZONI.

---

[1] *Non est dubium, quidquid in laudibus Matris proferimus, ad Filium pertinere, et rursum cum Filium honoramus, a gloria Matris non recedimus.* (St. Bernard, Homil. IV, *super Missus est*).

PART I

THE VIRTUES OF MARY IN
RELATION TO GOD

———

VIRGO FIDELIS.

Cor ejus fidele. 2. Efd. 9.

Mulier fide ... lis 1. Cor.

Efto fidelis usque ad mortem. Ap. 2.

CHAPTER I

MARY'S FAITH

1. Let us begin by considering in our Blessed Lady those three virtues which are the very basis of our religion and are called the Theological Virtues because they have God for their special and immediate object. These are Faith, Hope and Charity. Faith comes first, because without it we cannot please God, and he who draws nigh unto God must first of all believe.[1]

The first to extol the faith of Mary was her cousin Saint Elizabeth, who in her salutation declared her to be blessed for her faith. "Blessed art thou who hast believed."[2] She did not say "Blessed art thou because thou art

---

[1] Heb 11: 6.

[2] *Beata quae credidisti* (Lk 1: 45).

a daughter of David," or "because thou art a virgin," or even "because thou art the Mother of God," but "Blessed art thou because thou hast believed!" And what did Mary believe? She believed the words of Gabriel, who had told her things divine, but incredible to natural reason. The holy priest Zachary had doubted the words of this same angel,[1] but Mary believed readily and simply, merely asking, "How shall this be done?"[2] Truly it was a deep mystery that she could remain a virgin and yet become a mother. But Mary knew that with God all things are possible,[3] and with her lively faith she yielded assent to the angel's words. She only asked how she might at once and the same time observe her vow of virginity and obey the heavenly invitation. "How shall this be done?" *Quomodo fiat istud?* "How shall I become a mother? I am indeed espoused to a man, but he is for me only the associate in my vow. No other bond unites us. The prophet Isaias has indeed foretold that a virgin shall conceive and bear a

---

[1] Lk 1: 18.

[2] *Quomodo fiet istud?*

[3] Lk 1: 37.

son.[1] But tell me, Angel of God, how shall this be done?" And now, behold, that angel who but lately chastened the unbelief of Zachary by depriving him of speech, now rewards Mary's faith by revealing to her that she will conceive the Holy One by the operation of the Holy Ghost and through the power of the Most High.

Truly it was a reward worthy of her faith! For in this our present state God rewards faith, not by removing its veils, but by bringing it further and further into the sacred obscurity of new and more sublime mysteries, so that the mind rises from one degree of faith to another.[2] The truth of the Holy Trinity was shown in some way in the dimness of the future to saints of the Old Covenant,[3] but this profound mystery was now for the first time clearly and solemnly revealed: it was unfolded to Mary in requital of her faith. "The Holy Ghost shall come upon thee, and the power of the Most High shall overshadow thee. And therefore the Holy One that shall be born of thee shall be called the

---

[1] Is 7: 14.

[2] *Ex fide in fidem* (Rom 1: 17).

[3] Col 2: 17.

Son of God."[1] O ever-blessed Mary, who hast believed and by thy faith hast become Mother of Him who is Saviour of us all!

2. Mary's faith was not a transient act, lasting but for that instant in which she yielded assent to the angel's words. Her whole life was a continual exercise of faith. In truth since Mary was honoured by God with prerogatives not merely sublime but incomparable, she must needs, as long as she was a pilgrim upon earth, dwell in the *light* and in the *darkness* of faith, amidst mysterious marvels ever succeeding one another within her and around her. She was herself a mystery, because, although she was a daughter of Adam, she was free from Adam's guilt, she was true mother and true maid, a mere creature and yet Mother of the Creator. She believed most firmly that He who was born of her in time had been generated from all eternity, that He who lay in the manger was Lord of the universe, that the weeping babe wrapped in swaddling clothes was the joy of paradise. He fled from Herod, and she believed Him to be King of kings. He was condemned

---

[1] *Spiritus Santus superveniet in te et virtus Altissimi obumbrabit tibi, ideoque et quod nascetur ex te Sanctum, vocabitur Filius Dei* (Lk 1: 35).

to death, and she believed Him to be the Judge of the living and the dead. He died on the cross, and she saw in Him the Saviour of mankind. If faith is the *evidence of things that appear not*,[1] surely Mary's faith far surpassed all of the saints of the Old Law, who were so highly exalted by St. Paul for their faith.[2] They believed what they had not seen. Mary believed things that seemed contradicted by the evidence of her senses. "Blessed art thou who hast believed."

3. The blessed in heaven have no faith, as they have no hope, because one believes in what is not seen, and one hopes for what he does not possess, whereas the blessed in heaven now see clearly that in which they once believed, and they possess what was once the object of their hopes. Yet faith has a blessedness of its own, a blessedness peculiar to those who believe while pilgrims upon earth. They are blessed precisely because they do not see and yet believe. "Blessed are they that have not seen and have believed."[3] On this account Simon Peter was

---

[1] Heb 11: 1.

[2] Heb 11.

[3] *Beati qui non viderunt, et crediderunt* (Jn 20: 29).

called blessed by our Lord,[1] and even more blessed was Mary for her faith. "Blessed art thou who hast believed." The beatitude of faith is not, strictly speaking, one of Christ's eight Beatitudes,[2] but it is necessarily presupposed by them. They can exist only in faith and by faith, for this is the beginning and the germ of man's justification,[3] it is also the source of all the Beatitudes of the Gospel.

Unhappy the man who believes not. He is already condemned.[4] But how blessed is the simplicity of faith! "I thank Thee, Father, Lord of heaven and earth, because Thou hast hidden these things from the wise and learned, and hast revealed them unto little ones."[5] A cold logical reasoning is an intellectual effort which wearies and torments the mind that without wings would fain soar even to the regions of divine mystery.[6] Faith on the other hand is

---

[1] *Beatus es, Simon Bar-Jona: quia caro et sanguis non revelavit tibi, sed Pater meus, qui in coelis est* (Mt 16: 17).

[2] Mt 5: 3–11.

[3] *Fides est humanae salutis initium, fundamentum et radix omnis justificationis* (Conc. Trid., Sess. VI, ch. 8).

[4] *Qui autem non credit, jam judicatus est* (Jn 3: 18).

[5] Mt 11: 25.

[6] *Qui scrutator est majestatis, opprimetur a gloria* (Prv 25: 27).

a repose of the soul in revealed truth, a rest most sweet, like to that of John as he leant on the breast of Jesus. This sweet repose of faith was habitual to Mary. She remained at peace in the possession of revealed truth and guarded jealously the secrets of heaven within her virgin breast. Once and once only the joys of faith which inundated her soul burst forth and inspired her heart and her lips with that canticle that can never be forgotten, wherein the "Blessed among women" foretold that all men for ever would call her blessed.[1]

4. But the ever-blessed Virgin was more than a faithful guardian of revealed truths and in particular of the mysteries of the Word Incarnate. It was she who taught these truths to the disciples after her Son's Ascension. The words of St. Anselm are well known: "Many things were revealed to the Apostles by Mary."[2] Indeed the first two chapters of St. Luke are redolent of the reminiscences of that blessed Mother who as life draws near its close must have found delight in recalling the sweet memories of Jesus' childhood. "Mary kept all

---

[1] *Beatam me dicent omnes generationes* (Lk 1: 48).

[2] *Multa eis per hanc (Miriam) revelabantur* (St. Anselm, *De Excellent. Virginis*, ch. 7).

these things, pondering them in her heart."[1] The miraculous conception of St. John, Gabriel's colloquy with Mary, her visit to Elizabeth, the mysteries of Bethlehem, the circumcision, the presentation in the temple, the hidden life at Nazareth, the loss and finding of the Child at Jerusalem—all these circumstances St. Luke narrated by divine inspiration, but he must have learnt them also from Our Lady's lips. He tells us that he wrote what he had heard from those who had been "eye witnesses from the beginning;"[2] but these particular facts could have been related only by the Mother of Jesus. Who knows how St. Luke and the other disciples and especially St. John felt their hearts burn within them with faith and love as they listened to the narratives and the teaching of Mary, who has been rightly called *magistra fides*, the teacher of the faith.[3]

---

[1] *Maria autem conservabat omnia verba haec, conferens in corde suo* (Lk 2: 19,51).

[2] *Qui ab initio ipsi viderunt* (Lk 1: 2,3).

[3] Cf. Canisius, *De Maria Deipara Virgine*, bk. 4, ch. 2.

CHAPTER II

MARY'S HOPE

5. From faith springs hope, which is a joyous expectation of future glory and of the means whereby it is to be acquired. Who has ever hoped for the future glory of paradise with expectation so calm, so well assured as that of Mary, who gave birth to the author of that glory? Who has ever trusted to the loving providence of our heavenly Father with greater confidence than Mary did, who was the daughter of that Father? Theologians tell us that God, in the first moment of Mary's conception, infused into her soul together with faith and charity, the glorious virtue of hope.[1] But even without much store of theology, we can easily gather from the Gospel how great

---

[1] Suarez, *De Mysteriis Christi*, disp. 4. sect. 2.

was the hope that filled Mary's soul with joy. At Nazareth, at Bethlehem, in the Temple, in Egypt, on Calvary, in days of sunshine and in days of gloom, the Gospel shows us Mary ever calm, radiant with peace and full of trust in the future, like one that lives in heaven and longs only for heaven. Hence we are led to believe that the God of hope [1] was ever speaking to her heart with ineffable reasonings and showing her that there were prepared for her, chiefly for her, "those things which eye had not seen nor ear heard,"[2] so that the expectation of these great rewards must have made even suffering seem to her even welcome and desirable. "It is good for me to adhere to my God, to put my hope in the Lord God."[3]

The just Simeon as he took the Infant Jesus into his arms felt all earthly desires die within him, and his hopes of heaven became so ardent that he burst forth into that canticle: "Now Thou dost dismiss Thy servant, O Lord,

---

[1] St. Paul (Rom 15) speaks of God as the *God of patience and consolation* (5:5), *the God of peace* (5:33), and the *God of hope* (5:13), because all these virtues come from God.

[2] 1 Cor 2: 9.

[3] *Mihi autem adhaerere Deo bonum est, ponere in Domino Deo spem meam* (Ps 72: 28).

according to Thy word in peace, because my eyes have seen Thy salvation."[1]   What then shall we say of Mary, who bore Jesus for nine months in her womb, and during His infancy carried Him day after day in her arms, knowing well that her possession of Him in time was a pledge that she should hereafter possess Him eternally? Assuredly, never did created being in the enthusiasm of hope exclaim with deeper meaning than Mary did: "I will rejoice in the Lord and exult in God, my Jesus."[2]

6.   Hope in God becomes more vigorous and more manifest in the bitterest trials of life, as it lovingly commits to God all care for self.[3] In this respect also the virtue of hope shone forth marvelously in Mary. Joseph, her spouse, is filled with doubt and anguish on her account. Yet she says nothing on the secret things she has heard from the angel. She is silent trusting in God that He will Himself reveal these profound mysteries to Joseph by other means.   The

---

[1] Lk 2: 29,30.

[2] *Ego autem in Domine gaudebo; et exultabo in Deo Jesu meo* (Hab. 3: 18).

[3] *Jacta super Dominum curam tuam, et ipsi te enutriet* (Ps 54: 22). *Omnem solicitudinem vestram projicientes in eum, quoniam ipse cura est de vobis* (1 Pet 5: 7).

people of Bethlehem refuse to give her shelter on the night of her Child's birth, but she utters no word of lament, she does but hope in God that He will provide for her the resting-place she needs. During the years of exile in Egypt her greatest consolation is her hope that God, despite the fierce hatred of an earthly king, will take care of her and take her back to the land of her fathers. At Cana the Incarnate Wisdom denies her the favour she asks. Her answer is a sublime act of hope in the goodness of God Incarnate, and it is rewarded by a miracle. In her grief for the sufferings of Jesus, in her desolation at His death, while the disciples have well-nigh lost all hope,[1] Mary rejoices in the sweet assurance of seeing ere long her Son risen and glorious. Are not the words of the angel ever ringing in her ears: "He shall reign over the house of Jacob for ever, and of His kingdom there shall be no end"?[2]

---

[1] During the three days after our Lord's death faith indeed was not entirely extinct in the hearts of the disciples (cf. Bellarmine, De Eccl. Milit., 3, ch. 17), but they showed not a sign of hope. The two disciples going to Emmaus were speaking about their disappointed hopes. Nos sperabamus, quia ipse esset redempturus Israel, etc. (Lk 26: 21).

[2] Et regnabit in domo Jacob in aeternum. Et regni ejus non erit finis (Lk 1: 32,33).

All ye who are afflicted, embittered and disheartened by adversity, consider the example of her who was the blessed among women, and learn from her to hope!

7. Our Blessed Lady has not only taught us to hope, but also it is she who quickens and fosters all our hopes, so that we love to call her "Mother of holy hope,"[1] and to greet her tenderly as "Our Hope."[2] Truly all our hope is centered in Jesus Christ, because in Him is all good, He being the author of life and of happiness.[3] But Jesus was given to us by Mary, and it is in harmony with God's mode of acting that as our hopes began in Mary and through Mary, so they should be fully realized in her and through her.[4] The saints have loved to think that all heavenly graces come to us from God through the instrumentality and intercession of

---

[1] *Mater sanctae spei* (Ecclus. 24: 24).

[2] *Spes nostra.* In the *Salve Regina.*

[3] *Expectantes beatum spem* (Tit 2: 13).

[4] *Per quam meruimus Auctorem vitae suscipere.* In the prayer: *Deus qui salutis aeternae*, etc.

Mary.[1] SS. Irenaeus,[2] Jerome,[3] Augustine[4] and
Bernard[5] agree in saying that as Eve brought us
death, so life is given to us through Mary. This
seems to be bold language, and yet if rightly
understood, it is theologically exact.

"Lady, thou art so great and so prevailing
   That he who wishes grace, nor runs to thee
   His aspirations without wings would fly."[6]

---

[1] The opinion that all graces come to us from God through
Mary was defended by St. Alphonsus Maria Liguori (*Riposta
ad un Anonimo*), who has shown that it is supported by the
authority of many of the Fathers of the Church.

[2] *Sicut Eva inobediens facta, et sibi et universo generi
humano causa facta est mortis, sic et Maria...et sibi et
universo generi humano causa facta est salutis* (St. Irenaeus
bk. 3 *contra Haeres*, ch. 22).

[3] *Mors per Evam, vita per Mariam* (St. Jerome, *ad Eustochium,
de Custodia Virginitatis*).

[4] *Eva occidendo obfuit: illa percussit, ista sanavit* (Serm. 18,
De Sanctis, attributed to St. Augustine).

[5] *In te Angeli laetitiam, justi gratiam, peccatores veniam
invenerunt in aeternum* (St. Bernard, in Serm. 2, *Pentecostes*).

[6]   Dante, *Paradisio* 33, 5.
   *"Donna, se 'tanto grande e tanto vali
   Che qual vuol grazia e a te non ricorre,
   Sua disïanza vuol volar senz 'ali."*

CHAPTER III

MARY'S LOVE FOR GOD

8. Charity, as we are told by St. John, consists in union with God, because "God is charity, and he that abideth in charity abideth in God and God in him."[1] Hence it is that our soul which believes in God by faith and tends toward Him by hope, is united with Him only by charity. Now charity united the soul of Mary so closely to God that there never has been union with God more intimate than hers, save only the hypostatic union of the humanity of Jesus Christ with the Divine Word.[2] This is the

---

[1] 1 Jn 4: 16.

[2] *Jure ergo Maria sole perhibetur amicta, quae profundisssimam divinae sapientiae, ultra quam credi valeat, penetravit abyssum; ut quantum sine personali unione creaturas conditio patitur, luci illi inaccessibili videatur immersa* (St. Bernard, Serm. in *Signum Magnum*).

meaning of the angel's salutation: "Hail, full of grace, the Lord is with thee."[1] The fullness of grace that is in thee, O blessed among women, has united thee to the Lord with a perfect union: "The Lord is with thee." In fact. Our Lord, when He came to dwell in Mary's womb and to take flesh of her, united Himself to her even physically. Mary was thus united to God in body as well as in spirit; she knew God not merely as others do, but only as the Mother of God can know Him. "My heart and my flesh have rejoiced in the living God."[2]

9. It is therefore in Mary's maternity that we must find the secret of her love for God. In truth, no love can equal that of a mother, and therefore no one loved God as did the Mother of God. That God should have willed to be Incarnate and to become the son of a woman, is a profound and adorable mystery of love. But that she who was raised to the dignity of the divine maternity should have loved her God with boundless affection, this indeed can be easily understood. We cannot think of maternity apart from love. But the divine maternity of

---

[1] Lk 1: 28.

[2] *Cor meum et caro mea exultaverunt in Deum vivum* (Ps 83: 3).

Mary is unique, and the love it inspired must be incomparable. This shows us that there is no exaggeration in the statement made by the theologians, that Mary's love of God surpasses all the love of all the saints. This thesis has been demonstrated by Suarez, who starts from this principle, that, since Mary is the Mother of God, it is incongruous to suppose that the love of such a Mother for such a Son is not the greatest possible.[1] Again, Albertus Magnus, after admitting that the precept of love of God is perfectly fulfilled only by the blessed in heaven,[2] hastens to add that it seems unworthy of God that no one should ever have loved Him perfectly on earth. If anyone, he continues, did so love Him in this state of pilgrimage, it was Mary.[3] The Church therefore in her liturgy, when she would fain find expression for the transports of Mary's love, found no words more appropriate than those of the spouse of the Canticles, who has no love, no thought save

---

[1] Suarez, *De Mysteriis Christi*, q. 37, a. 4, disp. 18, sect. 4.

[2] Cf. St. Thomas: *Et ideo plene et perfecte in patria implebitur hoc praeceptum (charitatis); in via autem implebitur, sed imperfecte* (*Summa Theologiæ* (*ST*) II-II, q. 44, a. 6).

[3] *Aut aliquis implet hoc praeceptum, aut nullus: si aliquis, ergo beatissima Virgo* (Albertus Magnus, *Sup. Miss.*, ch. 76).

for her Beloved, seeks Him alone, possesses Him alone. "My Beloved to me, and I to Him."[1] Mary's Beloved was her God.

10. The tender love for God which glowed in Mary's heart never manifested itself, as far as we know, by ecstasies or raptures, such as we read of in the lives of many saints whose natural strength was oftentimes overwhelmed or absorbed by the excess of divine love. Mary was familiar with the marvels of God, and that native energy of soul and body which belonged to the sinless Mother was not weakened by the vehemence of her love. No ecstasy is recorded of her by tradition save only that rapture of love in which she died, to pass from earth to heaven.[2] But that which at one and the same time manifested and increased the ardor of Mary's love for God was chiefly her generous

---

[1] *Delectus meus mihi, et ego illi* (Cant. 2: 16).

[2] Msgr. Gay has well said that Mary's life "bore a much closer resemblance to the life of Jesus than to the lives of the saints, His servants who followed Him afar off. But Jesus had no ecstasies on earth. Not even the Transfiguration was an ecstasy; but it was a revelation, which of His free will and in His mercy He once vouchsafed to His three principle apostles, a revelation of His true inner self." (*Mysteries of the Rosary. The Assumption*). Cf. Suarez, *De Myst. Chr.*, q. 38, a. 4, disp. 21, sect. 1.

fidelity in complying with all the commands and desires of God. No angel or man ever did God's bidding more exactly or more nobly than Mary did.[1] United most perfectly as she was with God and filled with God's presence, she knew no evil, but did all things well, as maiden, as spouse, as mother. Hence the Holy Scriptures, which do not mention a single miracle wrought by the Mother of God, record with loving care her acts of virtue. Her humble words of answer to the angel,[2] her poverty at Bethlehem,[3] her gentle words to Jesus in the Temple,[4] her kindly thoughtfulness for the guests at Cana,[5] her heroic fortitude at the foot of the cross,[6] her prayerfulness in the guest chamber[7]—all these are traits of those virtues which adorn the mantle of the king's daughter, whose glory is

---

[1] *Si diligitis me, mandata mea servate* (Jn 14: 15).

[2] *Ecce ancilla Domini* (Lk 1: 38).

[3] *Peperit filium suum...et reclinavit eum in praesepio* (Lk 2: 7).

[4] *Fili, quid fecisti nobis sic?* (Lk 2: 48).

[5] *Vinum non habent* (Jn 2: 3).

[6] *Stabat autem juxta crucem Jesu mater ejus* (Jn 19: 25).

[7] *Hi omnes errant perseverantes unanimeter in oratione cum...Maria Matre Jesu* (Acts 1: 14).

all within, in her soul ardent with faith, with hope and with love.[1]

———————

ARTICLE I

MARY'S CONFORMITY TO THE WILL OF GOD

11. To love God infinitely would not be to love Him too much. But God alone is capable of infinite love. Man must be content with loving Him as much as he can by the aid of divine grace, with all his powers of mind, will, and feeling.[2] A man loves God with his will when he brings all his desires into conformity with the divine will. He loves God with his understanding when it rises to Him on the

———————

[1] *Omnis gloria filiae regis ab intus, in fimbriis aureis circumamicta varietatibus* (Ps 44: 14).

[2] *Ex omnibus viribus suis* (Lk 10: 27).

wings of contemplation and prayer. He loves God with his sensitive nature when he burns with zeal for God's glory. These three forms of charity towards God we will now consider one by one as they are found in our Blessed Lady. Let us begin with the first, namely, conformity to the will of God.

12. It is by doing God's will that a created will gains sanctity and merit. Apart from this, there can be no true solid virtue.[1] From this we can understand why our Lord Jesus Christ never praised His Mother except for one thing only, namely, for receiving the Word of God and keeping it. This eulogy He publicly pronounced on her when a woman in the crowd, lifting up her voice, cried out: "Blessed is the womb that bore Thee." Jesus replied: "Yea, rather, blessed are they that hear the word of God and keep it."[2] The word of God is not merely the written word of sacred writers or

---

[1] *Non omnis, qui dicit mihi: Domine, Domine, intrabit in regnum coelorum; sed qui facit voluntatem Patris mei, qui in coelis est, ipse intrabit in regnum coelorum* (Mt 7: 21).

[2] *Quin immo beati, qui audiunt verbum Dei custodiunt illud* (Lk 11: 28). By these words our Lord did not deny that honour was due to His Mother, but allowed *why* her maternity was worthy of honour.

the spoken word of preachers. Every sign of
the divine will is a word of God, no matter how
that will be signified, by means of things or of
men or of angels, by some secret whisper to
the heart, or through outward circumstances.
Mary observed carefully every indication of
God's will, whatever it might be, treasured
it and obeyed. Jesus, therefore, without
disparagement to the glory which accrued to
Mary from her divine maternity and her loving
care of His infancy, wished to teach us that she
is worthy of praise and glory incomparable, not
so much because she is His Mother, as for the
devoted love wherewith she did the will of God.
Hence St. Augustine tells us that "her maternity
would have profited her nothing, had she not
borne Christ more truly in her heart than in her
womb."[1] What a lesson for the vanity of men!
If the title Mother of God would have availed
Mary nothing, had she been devoid of virtue
befitting her office, what can nobility of birth
or worldly titles profit men without goodness
of life?

13. To conform all our desires and

---

[1] *Materna propinquitas nihil Mariae profuisset, nisi felicius
Christum corde quam carne gestasset* (St. Augustine, *De
Sancta Virginitate*, ch. 3).

affections and every movement of our will to the will of God is, in the language of Scripture, to have a heart according to God's own heart.[1] Such was the heart of Mary. Though she was Mother of her Lord, she thought of herself only as His handmaid. "As the eyes of a maiden look unto the hand of her mistress" to know her behests,[2] so was Mary wholly occupied and considering and fulfilling the commands, nay, the very desires of God. "Behold the handmaid of the Lord, be it done to me according to thy word."[3] These few words are full of meaning; they reveal to us Mary's soul. *Behold*, I am ready for anything God asks of me. *Behold the handmaid*, who exults in the consciousness of her own nothingness. *Behold the handmaid of the Lord*, who rejoices in the nothingness of the creature in view of the infinite greatness of the Creator. *Be it done to me* as God pleases. I will serve God, not as a passive, senseless instrument, but with all my activity, with all the strength of my personal will. *Be it done*

---

[1] 1 Kgs 2: 35; 13: 14. Acts 13: 22.

[2] *Sicut oculi ancillae in manibus dominae suae, ita oculi nostri ad Dominum Deum nostrum* (Ps 122: 2).

[3] *Ecce ancilla Domini, fiat mihi secundum verbum tuum* (Lk 1: 28).

to me according to thy word. O holy angel of God! In thee I see God who sent thee. Thy word is for me a sign of His will, and therefore my soul with deepest reverence receives it; and with it I accept all that it implies, all the consequences, immediate or remote, foreseen or not foreseen by me. I consent not only to the Redeemer's birth, but also to all His sorrows, tears and shame, His passion and death, and all the sufferings of His Mother and His saints. "Behold the handmaid of the Lord, be it done to me according to thy word."[1]

14. The will of God is ever holy and perfect, and yet St. Paul distinguishes a kind of gradation in its acts and speaks of one of these as good, of another as better, and a third as best.[2] Not that there are really gradations in God: but the will of God is like the sun whose light increases to our view from dawn to full daylight and thence to the splendor of noon. Even so there are different degrees of heavenly light, inasmuch as our souls know God's will more or less clearly. But the Mother of God always beheld the light of God's will in its

---

[1] Cf. Paolo Perez, *I sette silenzi e le sette parola de Maria,* Second Word.

[2] *Voluntas Dei bona et beneplacens et perfecta* (Rom 12: 2).

meridian splendor, and as she knew it well, so she fulfilled it well. And surely, if ever anyone, after Christ, penetrated into the mind of God, it was Mary. She not only possesses in its fullness the gift of knowledge of divine things and the gift of wisdom, that is, the love of the truth, a love which proves itself by deeds,[1] but more than all this, she was the tabernacle and abode of the Incarnate Wisdom, which dwelt for nine months in her womb.[2] The Divine Word, the Holy Ghost, the angels, illumined Mary's soul with such a brilliant light to know God's will, that she, lost in the abyss of her own nothingness, could not but live a life of adoration and of love, with these words ever on her lips: "Behold the handmaid of the Lord, be it done to me according to thy word."

---

[1] *Non est dubitandum, quin B. Virgo acceperit excellenter donum sapientae et gratiam virtutum et etiam gratiam prophetiae* (St. Thomas, *ST* III, q. 27, a. 5, ad. 3).

[2] *Qui creavit me requievit in tabernaculo meo* (Ecclus 24: 12).

Coronemus nos rosis. Sap. 2.

ARTICLE II

MARY'S SPIRIT OF PRAYER

15. The love of God readily produces the spirit of prayer, whereby the soul ascends to God, speaks to Him, thinks of Him, longs after Him. This loving elevation of the mind to God[1] is the secret and most delightful occupation of

---

[1] *Oratio est ascensus mentis in Deum* (St. John Damascene, *de Fide orthodoxa*, bk. 3, ch. 24).

every soul that loves God. Hence words cannot express the delight our Blessed Lady took in prayer. She had lived in childhood within the precincts of the Temple where she had been accustomed to divine contemplation. Hence by habitual disposition of mind she always felt attracted to the contemplation of heavenly things. Thus she was never less alone than when she seemed to be in solitude, because then she could best hold colloquy with the angels and with God. Her sublime contemplation did not hinder her diligence in good works, but while busy with external tasks she treasured in her mind all the words and deeds of her Jesus and pondered on their mysterious meaning.[1] But more clearly than this, we may say that she never ceased to commune interiorly with Jesus, and that therefore her whole life was spent in alternate contemplation and prayer. In fact, Jesus and Mary loved each other without limit, and whether they were near or far away they were ever united in spirit. They conversed without interruption in the secret language of love, and in Mary this love took the form of

---

[1] *Conservabat omnia verba haec, conferens in corde suo* (Lk 2: 19,51).

adoration and of prayer to the Word Incarnate, whom she worshipped in the inmost sanctuary of her heart *in spirit and in truth.*[1]

16. But prayer to God in spirit and in truth is not offered only in silence with the interior and secret utterance of the soul: it also at times finds expression in the spoken word and outpours itself in thanksgiving or supplication or divine praise.

This second manner of praying was likewise habitual with Mary. The psalms and canticles of the prophets which she had learned in childhood must often have been on her lips; and to her devout psalmody have been applied the words of Scripture: "The voice of the turtle-dove has been heard in our land."[2] Besides these sacred hymns, who can say what strains of tenderest love the Mother of God poured forth day by day in prayer? Assuredly her vocal prayer was not, as ours too often is, a cold repetition of words learnt by rote. It was the ardor and energy of love finding expression in glowing words. It is true that one prayer only composed by Mary has come

---

[1] *In spiritu et veritate oportet adorare.* (Jn 4: 24).

[2] *Vox turturis audita est in terra nostra* (Cant. 2: 12).

down to us, namely the *Magnificat*, which is sung in the evening Office of the Church with solemn rite. How beautiful is the Magnificat! It has been and will be the subject of learned and elaborate commentaries; but it is beautiful also when understood in its obvious meaning, deep study apart, as a prayer of thanksgiving and praise. First of all, Mary thanks God for having had regard to the lowliness of His handmaid, and for the great things He has done in her, He who is the Almighty, the Holy One.[1] In this her thanksgiving she magnifies Him with all the ardour of her soul and in the exaltation of her lofty mind.[2] Next Mary extols and magnifies the power of God in bringing to naught the proud, the rich, the powerful, and His mercy which raises up the weak, the poor and the lowly, and especially Israel His servant according to the promises given to Abraham and to his seed for ever.[3] Here it is noteworthy

---

[1] *Quia respexit humilitatem ancillae suae: ecce enim ex hoc beatam me dicent omnes generationes. Quia fecit mihi magna qui potens est, et sanctum nomen ejus* (Lk 1: 48,49).

[2] *Magnificat anima mea Dominum, et exultavit spiritus meus in Deo Salutari meo* (Lk 1: 46,47).

[3] *Et misericordia ejus a progenie in progenies timentibus eum, etc.* (Lk 1: 50–55).

that in Mary's prayer thanksgiving and praise are inspired by humility. She thanks God for the priceless gifts He has bestowed on His handmaid. She praises Him for humbling the proud and exalting the lowly. Thus the Blessed Virgin penetrates into the abyss of her own nothingness and of the divine greatness, and hence her prayer was such as, to use the words of Scripture, must pierce the clouds and ascend even to the throne of the Most High.[1]

It will be said that the Magnificat is a hymn rather than a prayer. But every prayer that is uttered with the enthusiasm of faith and with all the energy of the soul, is a hymn to God. Such must have been all the prayers of God's Blessed Mother.[2]

17. It is always sweet to pray in secret and in solitude, whether one prays with words or with sighs, in meditation or in contemplation, provided only it be in spirit and in truth. There are times however when public and common prayer should be made. This kind of prayer was highly commended by our Lord, who said: "Where there are two or three gathered together

---

[1] *Oratio humiliantis se, nubes penetrabit* (Ecclus. 35: 21).

[2] *Eructabunt labia mea hymnum* (Ps 118: 171).

in My name, there am I in the midst of them."[1]
Mary gave us an example also of this kind of
prayer when she united herself with the faithful
members of the newly-founded Church in the
guest chamber at Jerusalem. The disciples,
men and women, were there gathered together
[2] to prepare themselves by prayer for receiving
the Holy Ghost, and Mary was praying with
them.[3] It was a solemn occasion. Assuredly,
the Holy Ghost, the Paraclete, must descend
upon the faithful, for the promise given by
Jesus could not fail.[4] Yet He would not descend
except in answer to prayer, which must be
earnest in proportion to the greatness of the gift
of Himself which He was about to bestow upon
the Church. Now the disciples were good and
simple-hearted, but they were still weak in their
faith. Who could give vigour and, one might
almost say, omnipotence to their prayers? The

---

[1] Mt 18: 20.

[2] There were 120 persons or thereabouts exclusive of the
women, for Jews in reckoning the number of persons present
in an assembly never counted the women. (*Erat turba simul
fere centum viginti* (Acts 1: 15).

[3] *Hi omnes erant perseverantes unanimiter in oratione cum
mulieribus, et Maria matre Jesu, et fratribus ejus* (Acts 1: 14).

[4] Jn 14: 16,26.

Holy Scripture tells us that they prayed "of one accord with Mary, the Mother of Jesus." She who had given to men their Redeemer through the operation of the Holy Ghost, must now through the merits of the Redeemer obtain for men the Holy Ghost. The Redeemer came to us from Mary's womb, and on her prayer must depend the last and most precious fruit of the Redemption, which was the Holy Ghost the Paraclete. Here we have another reason for giving to our Lady the glorious title of *Adjutorium redemptionis*.[1] Mary in the guest-chamber prayed to the Holy Spirit with the confidence that befits His Spouse. Human words are too weak to express the ardent love with which she besought Him for the favour which He could not deny her.

---

[1] Albertus Magnus *super Missus est*, ch. 53.

ARTICLE III

MARY'S ZEAL FOR GOD'S GLORY

18. Zeal for God's glory is the ardent desire of the saints, that God's holy name may be hallowed both by themselves and by others. This ardour is what makes men apostles, but it is also a consuming fire in all souls that love God, even though they live solitary and contemplative. So was it with Mary. She chose by preference and loved the interior delights of solitude, of silence and of prayer. But was it possible that she, Daughter of God the Father, Mother of God the Son, Spouse of God the Holy Ghost, should not burn with vehement desire that all mankind should glorify that Father, that Son, that Spouse? How often must she, while still a child in the Temple at Jerusalem, have prayed with ineffable longings for the advent of Him who was to come? How often must she have exclaimed with accents of love, "Drop down dew, ye heavens, from above, and let the clouds rain the Just One: let the earth be opened

and bud forth a Saviour."[1] At a later time in
her little cottage at Nazareth how often must
her thoughts have turned to her Son's future
Kingdom which, as Gabriel had foretold, was to
endure forever. Then she would rejoice as she
thought of the promised salvation of the Elect,
the conversion of sinners, the joy of angels, the
overthrow of demons and the redemption of the
world. How she must have loved to repeat the
Angel's words: "He shall reign over the house
of Jacob for ever, and of His Kingdom there
shall be no end."[2]

This zeal for God's glory which consumed
her within, became at times manifest also to
others. For instance, scarcely had the Son
of God become Incarnate in her womb when
she set out in haste to visit her relatives in the
distant mountainous country of Judea,[3] that
they might share in the blessings of the Divine
Child. Again at the marriage-feast of Cana,
Mary by her faith hastened the hour in which
Jesus should show forth His power.[4] Again, she

---

[1] Is 14; 8.

[2] *Et regnabit in domo Jacob in aeternum, et regnt ejus non
erit finis* (Lk 1: 32,33).

[3] Lk 1: 39.

[4] Jn 2: 3–9.

tarried with the apostles in the guest-chamber that she might lend to the supplications of the disciples the efficacy of her own prayer.[1] Faith, prayer, the love of Jesus, interior virtues were the weapons of Mary's zeal. It was not stern and menacing like that of Elias. No, it had the mildness and sweetness of the spirit of Jesus, who would not break the bruised reed or quench the smoking flax, for He would fain give life to all and sanctify all.[2]

But let us leave these general reflections, and consider in particular the two instances of Mary's zeal which have just been mentioned, namely, her visit to St. Elizabeth and her conduct at the marriage-feast of Cana. These two instances best show forth our Lady's zeal.

19. The Angel Gabriel had told our Lady that her cousin Elizabeth had conceived a son in her old age. The Blessed Virgin, in the enthusiasm of her love and joy, went to visit her and journeyed in haste till she came "into the hill country to a city of Juda. And she entered into the house of Zachary and saluted Elizabeth. And it came to pass that when Elizabeth heard

---

[1] Acts 1: 14.

[2] Mt 12: 20.

the salutation of Mary, the infant leaped in her womb. And Elizabeth was filled with the Holy Ghost."[1] This maiden of fifteen years to whom God in her womb gives lightness and agility, and who seems to be wafted by the breath of the Holy Spirit, goes in haste and stays not till she reaches the home on the mountainside where she finds and tenderly greets her aged relatives. Does not this incident prove the truth of those words, ever beautiful and deep in meaning: "He who loves, flies, runs and rejoices; he is free, he is not held"?[2] Mary's haste, a thing so unusual with her, is like that of the spouse in the Canticle, to whom it is said: "Arise, hasten, my beloved, my dove, my beautiful one and come."[3] Love and joy inundate her soul. Her maidenly timidity does not hinder her from undertaking the long journey. Her divine burden does not retard her as she ascends the steep mountain path. The grace of the Holy Spirit will allow no delay. Jesus hastens that He may sanctify His precursor; Mary hastens that she may

---

[1] Lk 1: 39–41.

[2] *Amans volat, currit et laetatur: liber est, et non tenetur* (*De Imitat. Christi*, bk. 3, ch. 5, n. 4).

[3] *Surge, propera, amica, mea, columba mea, formosa mea et veni* (Cant. 2: 10).

bring gladness to Elizabeth; and both are eager to impart ineffable favours.[1] This indeed is pure and genuine zeal for the glory of God, for it is love manifesting itself by deeds and overflowing from the abundance of the heart.[2] Mary, filled with God's presence and inspired by the Holy Ghost, feels herself constrained to communicate God to the souls of others. It is a supernatural impulse, felt only by those chosen souls which love much, and which before they quit the seclusion of the inner life, heap up treasures of virtue, of wisdom and of that sacred heavenly fire which cannot but diffuse itself to enlighten and purify the world.[3] Alas, how rare is this true zeal for the glory of God! Some men seem indeed to be wholly consumed with the love of others, and yet in them there is not a spark of the love of God. There is a false zeal, restless and meddlesome, which is love

---

[1] *Laeta pro voto, religiosa pro officio, festina pro gaudio, in montana perrexit. Quo enim jam Deo plena, nisi ad superiora cum festinatione contenderet? Nescit tarda molimina Sancti Spiritus gratia* (St. Ambrose 1 *in Lucam*).

[2] *Ex abundantia enim cordis os loquitur* (Lk 6: 45).

[3] *Ignem veni mittere in terram; et quid volo nisi ut accendatur?* (Lk 12: 49).

of self, not love of God. It is a flower, showy indeed, but yielding no fragrance.

20. The loving zeal which quickened Mary's steps in her journey to that city of Juda, was again manifested at the marriage-feast of Cana, where she prevailed on Jesus to hasten the hour in which He was to show His power by miracles. It is the holy eagerness of a zeal which cannot brook delay and which runs in the way of the divine commandments after the perfumes of Him who exulted as a giant to run His course.[1] Jesus Christ had as yet wrought no miracles, and His hour had not yet come.[2] But Mary knew that times and moments may be hastened by prayer. The time seemed long to her ere her Son should be glorified and men be saved, and she could not refrain from uttering those words so significant in their simplicity: "They have no wine."[3] These words hastened the time of our Lord's miracles and of the salvation of the world. How often are we in

---

[1] *Viam mandatorum tuorum cucurri, cum dilatasti cor meum* (Ps 118: 32).—*Post te curremus in odorem unguentorum tuorum* (Cant. 1: 3).—*Exultavit ut gigas ad currendam viam* (Ps 18: 6).

[2] *Nondum venit hora mea* (Jn 2: 4).

[3] Jn 2: 3.

need of the wine of truth, the wine of grace, the wine of spiritual joy, and thou, dear Mother, dost obtain all for us from Jesus by thy loving prayer.[1]

---

[1] *Illa (tua vox), vinum non habent, necessaria nobis est: defecit vinum in cadis nostris, vinum scilicet laetificans cor hominis... Calix in manu tua vini meri, amoris divini: dic, Domina mea, dic pro nobis Filio tuo: vinum non habent* (Sermon on the *Salve Regina*, attributed to St. Bernard).

PART II

THE VIRTUES OF MARY IN RELATION TO MEN

———

Te in utero novem menſibus portavi, et lac dedi,
et alui. 2. Mach. 7.

CHAPTER I

MARY'S LOVE FOR THE SACRED HUMANITY OF JESUS

21.   Hitherto we have been considering those virtues of our Blessed Lady which have God for their immediate object.   Let us now pass on to those virtues of hers that have closer reference to men.   These are, first, her charity toward men in general, and secondly her charity as directed towards herself in particular.

Mary's love for her fellow-men includes her love for her Son Jesus Christ, for the Church, and for all mankind.   As we have already spoken of her love for Jesus Christ as God, we shall merely say a few words in this place regarding her exceeding love for Him as Man.

22.   The Humanity of Jesus Christ is the

great means whereby men may be saved.[1] This is why Jesus Himself took so much complacency in His human nature as to love to call Himself the *Son of Man*.[2] For this same reason there is no devotion more solid or more ancient than that to the Humanity of Jesus. Mary Magdalen loved it, and still more perhaps St. John the Evangelist, the friend of Jesus,[3] was enamoured of it, who through his intimate union with the Humanity of Christ soared higher than all others in the contemplation of His Godhead, and who learned the secrets of the Divinity while he rested blissfully on the bosom of Jesus.[4] But never has that sacred Humanity been loved by another human heart with love so strong, so tender, so sublime as

---

[1] St. Thomas, *ST* I-II, q. 112, a. 1; III, q. 7, a. 1; q. 62, a. 5.

[2] Mt 8: 20; 12: 32; 16: 13; Mk 2: 10; 8: 31; Lk 5: 24; 6: 51; Jn 1: 51; 3: 13, & 50.—It is a remarkable fact that as Jesus Christ loved to call Himself the *Son of Man*, so also (as far as we know from the Gospel) He never gave to Mary the name of *Mother*, but always addressed her as *Woman* (mulier). Perhaps He wished thereby to intimate that Mary is *the Woman* (or, as we say, *Our Lady*), who has repaired the evils wrought by the sin of the first woman. Cf. Suarez, *De Mysteriis Christi*, disp. 1, sect. 1.

[3] Jn 13: 23; 19: 26; 21: 20.

[4] St. Augustine in *Joann. Tract.*, 36.

Mary's was. It was she who had given to Jesus His human life, she had wrapped Him, an infant, in swaddling-clothes, and had nourished Him with her milk, she had cherished Him with infinite tenderness till He came to riper age. In fine, Mary was His Mother. She was the more a Mother because she remained a Virgin. She was the more a Virgin because she had received fruitfulness through the power of the Holy Ghost. She was so perfectly His Mother that in the emphatic words of St. Augustine: "The flesh of Jesus is the flesh of Mary."[1] Who then can describe or even conceive Mary's loving worship of the Humanity of Christ? She adored It visibly present to her in the stable at Bethlehem; she adored It in Egypt and at Nazareth; and then during the three years of our Lord's public ministry, she adored It again whenever she saw her Son, as at Cana, at Capharnaum, at Jerusalem. Then after His ascension she still honoured Him in the relics which she treasured—things hallowed by His touch. Now she adores Him in heaven, seated by His side and exulting in His unending

---

[1] *Caro Jesu, caro est Mariae* (*De Asumptione Beatae Mariae Virginis*, inter opera Augustini).

happiness. "The Queen is at Thy right hand, in raiment of gold."[1]

23. But our Lady's loving, reverent worship of the sacred Humanity of Jesus Christ must in a special degree have been profound and rich in merits when during the latter years of her life she received her Jesus in Eucharistic communion. He had said: "Whosoever eateth Me, the same also shall live by Me."[2] Mary therefore as she drew new life from Him to whom she herself had given life, had better reason than St. Paul to exclaim in the exuberance of her supernatural life in Christ, "I live now not I, but Christ liveth in me."[3] Doubtless she was wont to communicate daily. Indeed it is probable that the apostles counseled all the faithful to receive daily the Bread of Life,[4] and we are told that they "were persevering in the communication of the breaking of the bread."[5] We can easily imagine the holy gladness with which day by day from early dawn Mary's heart expanded in ardent desires for the Eucharistic food. We can

---

[1] *Adstitit regina a dextris tuis in vestitu deaurato* (Ps 94: 10).

[2] Jn 6: 58.

[3] *Vivo autem, jam non ego, vivit vero in me Christus* (Gal 2: 20).

[4] Cf. Suarez in III, diss. 18, sect. 3.

[5] Acts 2: 42.

imagine the sweetness of the Heavenly Manna to her taste, and the modesty and tenderness with which she received within her breast the body and blood of her Jesus, the profound peace which flowed in upon her soul strengthened with the "corn of the elect and the wine that bringeth forth virgins."[1]   When Jesus had ascended into heaven, earth would have been but a desert for Mary, had she not still found her beloved in the Eucharist, that she might lean on Him and be inebriated with delights.[2]

---

[1] Zac. 9: 17.

[2] *Quae est ista, quae ascendit de deserto, deliciis affluens, innixa super dilectum suum?* (Cant. 8: 5)

CHAPTER II

MARY'S LOVE FOR
THE CHURCH

24.   One cannot love the Humanity of Jesus Christ without loving also His Church, which is pre-eminently His "work."[1]   St. Paul tells us[2] that the Church is a body of which Jesus is the head, the soul and the life.   Hence even as he is *anathema* who loves not Jesus Christ[3] so we may say that he is *anathema* who loves not Holy Church. The Mother of Jesus therefore must needs have loved the Church with a mother's love.   She saw the humble commencement of that Church in the stable of Bethlehem, where Jesus, Mary and Joseph

---

[1] 1 Jn 17: 4.

[2] 1 Cor 12: 27.

[3] 1 Cor 16: 22.

formed the first Christian family, welcomed by the angels, visited by poor shepherds, honoured by kings. She saw the Church baptized by blood on Calvary and again baptized in the Holy Ghost at Pentecost. While the Church was still in the state of infancy and but lately bereaved of the dear presence of Jesus, Mary's special task was to tend and nourish her with solace and instruction to the end that the faith of the Church might increase to that manly vigour which was soon displayed by the martyrs of Jerusalem and of Rome.

25. We may add, in the words of St. Augustine, that Mary is a beautiful figure of the Church.[1] As Mary is virgin and mother, so also is the Church. Mary became a mother by the power of the Holy Ghost: it is by the grace of the same Holy Ghost that the Church

---

[1] *Ipsa figuram in se sanctae Ecclesiae demonstravit* (St. Augustine, *De Symbolo ad Catechumenos*, Sermo alius, ch. 1, Migne edition).—St. Ambrose had already made the same observation: *Bene desponsata (Maria) sed virgo, quia est Ecclesiae typus, quae est immaculata, sed nupta. Concepit nos virgo de Spiritu, parit nos virgo sine gemitu* (St. Ambrose in *Lucam*, 2, 7, Migne edition: cf. 10, 134). Hence Honorius of Autun has well said: *Gloriosa Virgo Maria typum Ecclesiae gerit... Ideo cuncta quae de ecclesia scribuntur, de ipsa etiam satis congrue leguntur* (Honorius Augustod. *In Sigillo B.M.,* Migne edition).

gives birth to her children in Baptism. The Holy Spirit therefore is the Spouse of both Mary and the Church. But He is a spouse who does not tarnish but enhances and perfects their virginity. The mutual resemblance of these twin daughters of the Most High enables us easily to understand the immense love of the Church for Mary and Mary's most tender return of love. Are they not both crowned with the same glories, do they not grieve over the same griefs and are they not Queens of the same realm?

26. The Church, conscious of Mary's love, gratefully and gladly attributes to Our Lady all her own triumphs over heresy, and sings joyfully her Office: "Rejoice O Virgin Mary, thou alone hast overcome all heresies throughout the world."[1] These words of highest praise will not seem extravagant to one who reflects that Mary indeed destroyed in germ all the heresies that in time to come were to spring up among Christians, by giving to us Jesus Christ, whose heavenly doctrine was to dispel all darkness of error from the world. Besides we must

---

[1] *Gaude, Maria Virgo, cunctas haereses sola interemisti in universo mundo.* In the "Office of the Blessed Virgin Mary."

remember that Mary, after our Lord's ascension, lived many years on earth for the consolation and instruction of the newly founded Church.[1] Doubtless the apostles learnt from her how best to confute error and yet be tender with those that err. She must have disclosed to them the most hidden secrets of that doctrine with which they converted the world. Therefore has Mary been crowned in heaven *Queen of apostles*. Now from her heavenly home she is still the protectress of those who proclaim and defend the Christian Faith, and she exerts in their behalf the efficacy of her patronage. Indeed, at times, the manifestation of her power is likened to the might of an army ready for battle.[2]

---

[1] Suarez, on the testimony of ancient writers, considers it most probable that Mary died at the age of 72 (in III, q. 37, disp. 21, sect. 1).

[2] *Terribilis ut castorum acies ordinata* (Cant. 6: 9).

DOMUS AUREA.

CHAPTER III

MARY'S LOVE FOR MANKIND

27. The Church is the mystical Body of Jesus
Christ, and all men are invited to become
members thereof. Hence it is impossible to
love sincerely Jesus and the Church without
loving also the whole human race. Suffice it
to say of Mary's love for mankind that she is

the *co-redemptrix*, the *mother* and the *advocate* for all men.

28.   Mary is *co-redemptrix*.   Jesus and Mary: these are the two dear names with which the entire plan of our salvation is entwined. This was the will of God, that as a man and a woman were the authors of our ruin, so a man and a woman should bring us salvation.[1] As Jesus Christ is the Redeemer of mankind, Mary was destined to be the co-redemptrix, or, to use the phrase of Albertus Magnus, *Adjutorium redemptionis*. Jesus Christ is verily the Redeemer of mankind, but He has been given to us by Mary. She is therefore of necessity our co-redemptrix. When we speak of redemption, we picture to ourselves the Divine Victim hanging on the cross. And yet the mystery of the cross is not to be separated from the mysteries of the crib, for the Evening Sacrifice of Calvary was but the completion of the Morning Sacrifice of the Incarnation. The priceless Victim offered on the cross had been prepared and fashioned in Mary's womb. The heroines of Israel, Abigail who saved her

---

[1] Cf. St. Irenaeus, *Adv. Haereses*, III, 22; St. Augustine, Serm. 13, and 17; St. Sophronius, Homil. In *Deiparae Annunutiat*.

husband, Judith who saved a city, Ester who saved her people, were but faint images of her who brought into the world the Saviour not of a man, not of a city, not of a nation, but of a whole human race. *Adjutorium redemptionis*.

29. *Mary is the mother of men.* They had been betrayed by Eve, unworthy of the name of mother. They had need of a mother who would love them, and they have found her in Mary. She is the Mother of Jesus Christ, who, as St. Paul tells us, is our Elder Brother.[1] We are therefore Mary's younger children. Jesus belongs to her by nature, we are hers by adoption. As we are by adoption sons of God, so we are likewise adopted children of Mary. Our adoption as sons of God was bought by the blood shed on the cross of Calvary, and it was on Calvary through that same stream of blood that we received our adoption as children of Mary. For the First-born as He hung on the cross said to the whole family of the redeemed, represented by John: "Behold thy Mother."[2] Mary therefore loves each one of us not merely as her neighbor, but as a most dear child. She

---

[1] Rom 8: 29.

[2] Jn 19: 27.

loves us all, because all are called to be brothers of Jesus and all are loved by Jesus. Mary in giving birth to our Lord, had not experienced the pains of the first Eve, but she did experience them in becoming the mother of men, in order that she might with full truth be called the second Eve, even as Jesus is the second Adam. The pains of travail were merited by Eve under the tree of death, and were endured by Mary in nobler child-birth at the foot of the tree of life, where she suffered for all who were to be her spiritual children. Ah, let us not forget the sorrows of this dear Mother![1]

30. *Mary is the advocate of men.* She fulfills perfectly the duties of the loving mother of all mankind, and as the hen gathers her chickens under her wings, so Mary protects her children by her intercession and prayers. Do not the saints in heaven powerfully intercede for us because they are friends of God and our brethren? Shall not then Mary be our advocate, who is at once Mother of God and our mother? Therefore we have recourse to her every day and with the Catholic Church salute her as our advocate. On this subject

---

[1] *Gemitus matris tuae ne obliviscaris* (Ecclus. 7: 29).

St. Bernard writes thus: "Thou art awestruck even by hearing the voice of the Father, thou art ashamed to approach Him and wouldst fain hide thyself among the trees of the garden. Lo! He hath given thee Jesus for a Mediator... But perchance thou shrinkest before the Divine Majesty in Him also, since albeit He be made Man, He remaineth still God. Wouldst thou have an advocate with Him likewise? Have recourse to Mary. There is nothing in Mary but pure humanity—pure, not only in the sense of being free from any kind of contamination, but in that of being pure and simple human nature and nothing more. And I have no hesitation in saying that she also will be heard on account of her reverent submission. The Son will indeed hear the mother, and the Father will hear the Son."[1]

---

[1] *Ad Patrem verebaris accedere; solo auditu territus, ad folia fugiebas: Jesum tibi dedit mediatorem... Sed forsitan et in ipso majestatem vereare divinam, quod, licet factus sit homo, manseit tamen Deus? Advocatam habere vis et ad ipsum? ad Mariam recurre. Pura siquidem humanitas in Maria, non modo pura ab omni contaminatione, sed pura singularitate naturae. Nec dubius dixerim, exaudietur et ipsa pro reverentia sua. Exaudiet utique matrem Filius. Exaudiet Filium Pater* (St. Bernard, serm. *de Nativitate B.V.M.* See the Roman Breviary, translated by John Marquess of Bute Vol. 1, p. 1454).

ARTICLE I

MARY'S LOVE FOR HER SUPERIORS

31. Hitherto we have been considering Mary's love for all men in general. Now we must speak in detail about the manifold virtues which were the effects and evidence of this, her love. While she lived on earth, she loved her superiors, her equals, her inferiors, friends and foes, all mankind. She was ever obedient to those above her, benign to her inferiors, amiable to her equals; she showed mercy to the wretched; she gave edification to all. Let us first speak of Mary's obedience.

32. The loving obedience of children to their parents and of the wife to her husband is the condition on which the good order of the family depends, as we are told by St. Paul.[1] In the Holy Family, the model of perfect domestic society, Mary humbly obeyed Joseph, and Jesus obeyed both.[2] The father of the family has a right to command, and it is by him

[1] Eph. 5: 21,22.

[2] Lk 2: 51.

that God makes known His will to the entire household. To Joseph therefore was given the Angel's warning when they must flee into Egypt, and likewise to Joseph was made known the day of their return. "He took the Child and His Mother by night and went into Egypt:"[1] and again: "He took the Child and His Mother and came into the land of Israel."[2] What an example of obedience! Jesus and Mary allow themselves to be led away in the night, they ask not whither! Certainly Joseph knew whither they were going, but the Gospel does not tell us that Jesus and Mary were told. Yet Joseph was well aware that in the sight of God he was the least worthy to govern that Holy Family. He ruled therefore with humble diffidence, while Jesus and Mary obeyed him with admirable humility. In truth, humility is needful not only for obeying but also for commanding well, since it sometimes happens that one who is subject has greater virtue than his superior, who has reason therefore to abase himself in spirit.

33. Our Lady gave also a luminous

---

[1] Mt 2: 14.

[2] Mt 2: 21.

example of obedience to the civil authority.[1] The Emperor Augustus had issued an edict that a census should be taken of the whole world, including the allied and tributary kingdoms, one of which was Palestine. "And Joseph also went up from Nazareth, a city of Galilee, into Judea to the city of David, called Bethlehem, because he was of the house and lineage of David, that he might be enrolled with Mary his espoused wife who was with child."[2] Mary was young, poor and with child. Certainly this journey of some fifty miles, from Nazareth to Bethlehem, over rough roads, in winter time, was for her no little trial. But the edict of Augustus had been promulgated to all his subjects.[3] Mary therefore obeyed for conscience's sake[4] without complaint, without delay. God had promised that the Saviour should be born at Bethlehem, the city of David,[5] but Mary His predestined Mother, dwelt at Nazareth. How

---

[1] The duty of obedience to civil authority is plainly taught in
   Mt 17: 25,26; 22: 17–21; Lk 22: 25,26; Rom 13: 1–5.

[2] Lk 2: 4,5.

[3] It was the custom of the Romans to include the women in
   the Census. Cf. Livy bk. III, ch. 3.

[4] Rom 13: 5.

[5] Mi 5: 2.

then should she give Him birth in the far-off Bethlehem? The decree of the Roman Emperor is the occasion of Mary's performing the act of obedience which was needed for the fulfillment, according to prophecy, of the design of the almighty.

34. As in the family and in the civil society there is an authority which we must obey, so also in the religious society of the Church there are superiors to whom we must render the homage of loving obedience.[1] We might speak of the dutiful submission which Mary, while yet a child, yielded to the ministers of the sanctuary and to the matrons who had care of her. But let it suffice us to mention the sublime obedience practiced by our Lady on the day of her purification. Moses had ordained[2] that every woman for forty days after child-birth should be forbidden to touch holy things, and be excluded, as one impure, from the Temple until the day of her purification. On the fortieth day after the birth of the child, the mother was to come to the Temple and make an offering

---

[1] *Obedite praepositis vestris et subjacete eis. Ipsi enim pervigilant quasi rationem pro animabus vestris reddituri, ut cum gaudio hoc faciant, non gementes* (Heb 13: 17).

[2] Leviticus 12.

of a lamb one year old and a turtle-dove or a pigeon, or if she was poor, she might offer two turtle-doves or two young pigeons, the one as a holocaust and the other for her purification. Accordingly, Mary, ever obedient to the priests and to the law, came to the Temple to be purified. She was poor, and therefore she brought two doves or young pigeons, the offering of the poor; but in fact she offered the true Lamb, who forty days before had been born of her and had been laid on the hay of the stable. She presented herself to the priests amidst mothers defiled by sin, though she was Queen of Virgins, purer than angels and Mother of God. O marvel of obedience! Mary has heard the praises of Gabriel and of Elizabeth, she has been inspired to sing her prophetic hymn *Magnificat*, she has received homage from the shepherds and the kings. Yet she now abases herself in profound submission to the common humiliation of her sex. Might she not have said that *God had done great things in her womb* and that *blessed was the fruit of her womb* and that the immaculate maiden had no need of purification?[1] Ah, Mary

---

[1] *Cum in omnibus matribus non fiat sine peccati sorde conceptio, haec (Maria) inde purgationem traxit unde concepit* (St. Leo the Great, Serm. 2, *De Nativ. Domini*).

was not one to think of her privileges! As she would have foregone the honour of divine maternity in order to remain a virgin, so now rather than display her prerogatives, she prefers to seem to be as the rest of women. She would rather be the humble handmaid of God and His ministers, than reveal the glory of her virginity.

———

ARTICLE II

MARY'S LOVE FOR HER INFERIORS

35. Charity towards one's inferiors takes the name and the form of benignity. This virtue has a charm all its own. The superior who possesses it, draws to himself the love of those whom he rules, and they are happy to obey. But who was subject to Mary? She was the humblest of God's creatures, and while she lived on earth

was in subjection to all: to her parents Joachim and Anna, to Joseph her spouse, and finally to the apostles as her pastors, and above all to St. John her guardian. O heavenly mystery! Mary, subject to all human creatures, ruled the Son of God! No one was under her authority, save Jesus Christ who yielded obedience to her and to Joseph.[1] Assuredly never did monarch hold more glorious sway than Mary did over her one Subject,[2] and never was rule so benign and enviable as Mary's was. Indeed, who can describe or even conceive the tenderness of a mother, wherewith Mary gave her commands to her Subject? That we may understand something of it, the Holy Scripture has recorded her gentle words to Jesus when after three days' loss and anxious search she found Him in the Temple among the doctors. "Son, why hast thou done so to us? Behold Thy father and I have sought Thee sorrowing."[3] How tender are these words, not of reproof but of enquiry! Why hast Thou done so to us? A question asked quietly and

---

[1] *Erat subditis illis* (Lk 2: 51).

[2] *Deus...cui Angeli subditi sunt, cui Principatus et Potestates obedient, subditus erat Mariae* (St. Bernard, hom. 1, *super Missus est*).

[3] Lk 2: 48.

gently is usually far more modest, delicate and affectionate than an assertion, which oftentimes has in it something harsh, stern and peremptory. Moreover, the word *Son*, while it expresses Mary's authority over her Child, contains the loving complaint of her maternal tenderness, with the consciousness of Jesus' return of filial piety. Then the words "Thy father and I have sought Thee sorrowing," manifest her regard for her spouse. Mary has no jealousy of his authority. She names him first, with the title *father*, though he was only the reputed and adoptive father of Jesus. In fine, we admire in Mary's words, authority with humility. Her complaint is just, but without bitterness. Her words are noble and tender, such as befitted the Mother of such a Son. Love was the secret of Mary's rule. It was the life and spirit of the Holy Family. It was love supernatural in Mary who ruled, love divine in Jesus who obeyed.

36. But Mary's benignity towards those beneath her is even more clearly evinced now that she reigns as Queen in heaven by the side of Jesus Christ. Paradise is called the Kingdom of Heaven, and therefore all the saints who have inherited that realm are kings. But since

in heaven dignities are conferred in proportion to merit, Mary, who is the most holy of all saints, is Queen over all the kings in paradise, Queen of angels, patriarchs, prophets, apostles, martyrs, confessors and virgins. She reigns with Christ over us also, who are exiles and pilgrims upon earth, and therefore we salute her every day as our Queen. *Salve Regina!* This most gracious Queen was called by St. Bonaventure the "Ravisher of hearts."[1] This title is most appropriate and expressive of Our Lady's gracious benignity. Gladly we bend our knees before her to entreat her lovingly to cast on us one glance of her eyes. *Salve, regina... illos tuos misericordes oculos ad nos converte.* Happy he who can win one look from this Queen! As the eyes of the handmaid are directed to the hand of her mistress, even so are our eyes ever fixed on thee, O Mary![2]

---

[1] *O raptrix cordium, quando mihi restitues cor meum?* (*Stimuli divini amoris*, part 3, ch. 19 [a work once attributed to St. Bonaventure. Editor's note]).

[2] *Sicut oculi ancillae in manibus dominae suae, ita oculi nostri* (Ps 122: 2).

ARTICLE III

MARY'S LOVE FOR HER EQUALS

37. Amiability towards one's equals is a virtue which attracts less notice than does obedience to superiors or benignity to inferiors, and yet perhaps it is more rarely found. St. Ambrose in his enumeration of the virtues of Mary ever Virgin does not omit to touch upon her goodness toward her equals, but he indicates only its negative quality.[1] Mary's amiability in dealing with her equals was not mere freedom from envy, *non invidere*, but rather it was the charm of her gentle words, her self-adaptation to the ways and disposition to others, and the careful heed she paid to times, places and persons. In fine, she showed towards all that

---

[1] *Aequalibus non invidere.* The second chapter of the second book of St. Ambrose's treatise *De Virginibus* contains one of the most complete eulogies of Mary's virtues that are to be found in the writings of the Fathers. St. Ambrose fitly mentions among her virtues: *nullum laedere, bene velle omnibus, assuregere majoribus natu, aequalibus non invidere, fugere jactantiam, etc.* (*De Virginibus*, n. 7).

courtesy and love which give charm and ease to human intercourse.

38. It is true that we have not those minute details of Mary's private life which alone could portray her to us in her winning ways with her relatives and friends. But it is certain, that she never moved the women of Nazareth to envy or jealousy by displaying her prerogatives. She lived unnoticed, making herself like in all things to the other women, who called her the mother of Jesus[1] but knew nothing of the incomparable dignity of Mother or of Son. In treating with her relatives she was always affable and kind. At the marriage-feast of Cana in Galilee we see Mary with Jesus sharing the rejoicings of the spouses and their relatives and friends. Mary, though a virgin who cared not for worldly pleasures, was bright and joyous at those nuptials, for she would not separate herself unnecessarily from others, and she wished to show proper deference to the claims of kindred. But in the midst of the innocent mirth and feasting the wine failed. Mary with delicate perception knew how to combine

---

[1] *Nonne hic est fabri filius? Nonne mater ejus dicitur Maria, etc.* (Mt 13: 55; Mk 6: 3).

affection for her relatives with ardour for God's glory. She who had not once during thirty years asked Jesus for a miracle to gratify herself, now feels gently constrained to ask such a favour for others. Her petition obtains from Jesus that wonderful wine which, while it fills the guests with new and mysterious gladness, strengthens the disciples in their faith.[1]

39. It is generally believed that during the three years of our Lord's public ministry, Mary followed her Son, in company with the pious women who ministered to Jesus of their substance.[2] Also in this Mary did not bring herself into notice, but merely conformed to the national custom, which was that women should render such services to persons of authority.[3] But it was a sight to move the admiration of the angels to see God's own Mother passing from place to place in the company of poor women,[4] and demeaning herself like them

---

[1] Jn 2: 2.

[2] Lk 8: 3.

[3] *Consuetudinis Judaicae fuit...ut mulieres de substantia sua victum atque vestitum praeceptoribus ministrarent.* (St. Jerome, *Comm, in caput 27 Matt.*).

[4] The Gospel has recorded the names of these women, but perhaps there were many others (Lk 8: 2,3).

in the rendering of the humblest services. Methinks the daughter of Jefte who for two months wandered with her companions among the mountains to bewail her virginity[1] is far less pathetic a figure than the Virgin Mother, who during the space of three years goes with the pious women from town to town, from village to village, that she may tend the Divine Master with ineffable love.

———

ARTICLE IV

MARY'S LOVE OF COMPASSION

40. Among the manifold forms of Mary's love for mankind, we cannot pass over in silence that most attractive form of love, ever ready to aid the afflicted, which we call

---

[1] Jgs 11: 37,38.

the mercy of compassion. Mary's deeds of mercy at Nazareth and Bethlehem, in Egypt and elsewhere during her mortal life, are but little known to us. Yet it is certain that she had the same compassionate heart which she has now in heaven, a heart full of tenderness for the unhappy children of Eve, the heart of the Mother of mercy, *Mater misericordiae,* Indeed we daily salute her as *Health of the sick, Refuge of sinners, Comfort of the afflicted.* In every evil, physical, intellectual, or moral, that crosses our path, we implore the aid of Mary.

41. *Salus infirmorum.* Here I will say but little of the miraculous cures of all kinds of diseases obtained in times past and in our own days through Mary's intercession. Granted that many alleged occurrences are apocryphal, it is not reasonable to refuse credence to the many facts which are attested by the strongest evidence. We know that virtue went forth from Jesus to heal all diseases.[1] Can we then be surprised that His Mother's prayers should have power to heal? If the shadow of St. Peter falling on the sick could give them health,[2]

---

[1] *Virtus de illo exibat, et sanabat omnes* (Lk 6: 19).

[2] Acts 5: 15.

how much more potent must be the prayer of the Mother of God? But—leaving miracles aside—Christians instinctively have recourse to Mary in times of illness, when the body is in pain and the mind is full of fears. She is wont to grant them ineffable consolations: often she strengthens them to patience: sometimes she alleviates their sufferings. But in all physical evils the most tremendous is the agony of death, and for this we prepare ourselves every day by saying to Mary: *Pray for us now and at the hour of our death.* Mary, seated by the death-bed of St. Joseph, made death itself seem sweet to him. She, standing beneath the cross, beheld her Son's cruel death on Calvary. She will be propitious to us also in our last moments, *in hora mortis nostrae.*

42. *Refulgium peccatorum.* Alas, we are beset by other evils, worse than those of the body. Our guilty passions, avarice, concupiscence, ambition and anger, are more deadly to the soul than any fever can be to the body.[1] In one word, sin is the fever that kills the soul. But though we are sinners, we may find

---

[1] *Febris enim nostra, avarita est: febris nostra, libido est: febris nostra, luxuria est: febris nostra, ambitio est: febris nostra, iracundia est* (St. Ambrose, ch. 4, *in Lucam*, 4).

safety in the compassion of Mary, the refuge
of sinners. As Jesus is the good shepherd
who makes his way over the rugged heights
of the mountains in quest of the lost sheep, so
the Mother of Jesus is like the woman in the
gospel who lights her candle and searches the
whole house to find the groat she has lost. In
truth we children of wrath have cost Mary
something more precious than money. Did
we not cost her all that stream of blood that
flowed on Golgotha? That blood had come to
Jesus from Mary and from her alone, and she
offered it with Him on that fearful Mount for
the salvation of sinners. If then we are sinners
and prodigals, far from God and fearful of His
wrath, if we feel the biting fang of remorse, and
tremble for our salvation, let us as penitents
have recourse to Mary. We shall receive from
her the mother's love and the peace for which
we crave. Indeed, Mary on the day that her
Divine First-born died on the cross, suffered
the unspeakable pains of a mystical childbirth
and brought forth her younger children without
number. As she had become the Mother of
God without ceasing to be a virgin, so now she
became mother of sinners without ceasing to be

the Mother of God. If then filial reverence or natural shame keeps us back from approaching the Father whom we have offended, let us be of good heart and fly to our Mother. *Surgam, et ibo ad matrem*. Thou hast not known sin, O Mother, and yet thou art the loving mother of sinners. "Be thou unto me a house of refuge, that thou mayst save me."[1]

43. *Consolatrix afflictorum*. There are innumerable persons who are unhappy in this vale of tears. To the sick and the sinful must be added many others who are in misery, deprived of all gladness and distressed by family troubles or public calamities or their own personal misfortunes. To all these Mary offers her loving consolation: *Consolatrix afflictorum*. When we read in the Gospel that an infant in the womb leapt for joy at the sound of Mary's voice,[2] we may easily imagine the tranquil gladness that must have been manifest in our Lady's looks and acts and words while yet she dwelt on earth, gladness which could not fail to communicate itself to the souls of all who approached her in time of trial or affliction. Of Judith it was said

---

[1] *Esto mihi…in domum refugii, ut salvum me facias* (Ps 30: 2).

[2] *Ecce enim ut facta est vas salutationis tuae in auribus meis, exultavit in gaudio infans in utero meo* (Lk 1: 44).

that she was the *joy of Israel*, but this glorious title is far better applied to Mary. Thou art *the joy of Israel*.[1] If Mary brought joy to men during her mortal life, what shall we say of her now that she is enthroned as Queen of heaven? This is why devotion to our Lady is recommended as a means of restoring serenity to a saddened and gloomy mind. At the very thought of Mary the spirit becomes tranquil and darkness is dispelled from the mind. The mention of her diffuses joy. The invocation of her name gives new courage, even in moments of despondency and of conflict, and puts our foes to flight. Therefore one of the noblest titles we give to Mary is that of *Causa nostra laetitiae*. In truth, the "Joy of all the earth" is our Lord and Saviour Jesus Christ, but Mary is His Mother, and therefore is rightly called the *Cause of joy: Causa nostra laetitiae.*[2]

---

[1] *Tu laetitia Israël* (Jdt 15: 10).

[2] *Gaudium universae terrae* (Lam 51: 15).

MATER AMABILIS.

Amabilis super amorem mulierum. 2 Reg. 1.

ARTICLE V

MARY'S LOVE FOR ALL MEN

44. We must now bring to a close our considerations on Mary's love for men; and as we have spoken of her love for the Sacred Humanity of Jesus Christ, for the Church, for her superiors, her equals and those beneath her, and in particular for all who are in affliction or distress, we shall conclude by saying that

she loved all mankind, and practiced that all-embracing virtue which each one of us can and should cultivate, namely, the virtue of edification. Had Mary conferred no other benefit on men than the edification of her example, she would have deserved the eternal gratitude and admiration of the human race. It is true that the Gospel narrative is silent regarding the influence which our Lady's example exercised over others, but we can easily form some notion of it from her work in later times. It is her example that has inspired innumerable maidens with the love of virginity. So many other saints have taken as their model her humility, generosity, charity and other virtues, and have drawn from her example light and strength to attain unto the heroism of Christian wisdom.

45. The virtue of edification is that *good odor of Christ* which is diffused by those who faithfully render themselves like to Him.[1] Indeed, when we witness some good act of virtue, we seem to feel the presence of Christ and to inhale its divine fragrance, or at least we are moved to turn our thoughts to Him and

---

[1] *Christi bonus odor sumus* (2 Cor 2: 15).

to *run after the odours of His perfumes.*[1] But where can we find this celestial fragrance so rich as in Mary the Mystical Rose, that contained for nine months the virtue of the Humanity of Christ? Tertullian has said that the body of the first man as fashioned by the Creator showed, as it were, the faint outlines of the features of the Christ who was to come.[2] But we may also say, and even with greater propriety, that there never was a more faithful likeness of Jesus Christ than that which was seen in Mary His Mother, and that on seeing her, one thought of Jesus Christ. *Christus cogitabatur.* Those who looked on her even in the days of her mortal life, beheld as in a mirror the image of her Son Jesus. They saw in her the sweetness, modesty, charity and beauty of the Son of Man, and as they gazed on her, they might have used the poet's words with more subtle meaning than he had given them: "Such were his looks, his gestures, his mien."[3]

46. He who would fain study our Blessed Lady as a type of perfection, should read what

---

[1] Cant. 1: 3.

[2] *Quodcumque limus exprimebatur, Christus cogitabatur homo futurus* (Tertullian, *De Resurrectione carnis*, n. 6).

[3] *Sic oculos, sic ille manus, sic ora ferebat* (Virgil *Aen.*, III, 490).

St. Ambrose says of her. "Let the life of the Virgin Mary be ever present to your mind as a mirror of chastity and of every virtue, that you may copy her example and learn from her what to think, what to do, what to avoid. The excellence of the teacher is an incentive to learning; but who is more excellent than the Mother of God? Who is more resplendent than she who was chosen by Splendour itself? Who is purer than she who was conceived undefiled? But what should I say of her other virtues? She was a virgin in body and mind, for no unworthy affection ever lessened the ardour of her love for God. Mary was humble of heart, grave in speech, prudent in mind, sparing in her words and given to reading. She set her hopes not on transitory wealth but on the prayers of the poor. She was ever intent on her work, modest in speech, accustomed to look not to man but to God as the judge of her thoughts. To offend no one, wish well to all, revere her elders, have no envy of her equals, flee from vainglory, follow reason and love virtue, these merits were hers in a singular degree. When did Mary even by a glance show disrespect to her parents? When had she dissensions with her kindred? Or when did she condemn the abject, or deride the weak, or turn with disgust from the poor? Mary saw nothing of men save when she could do some kind act of charity without repugnance to her virgin modesty. The Virgin Mother had no sternness in her looks, there was no boldness in her words, no immodesty in her acts. Her gestures were seemly, her movements quiet and dignified, her voice gentle and low, so that her external deportment betokened the serenity and nobility of her soul and reflected its goodness... What shall I say of Mary's temperance in the use of food and of the regard she showed to everyone? She multiplied her fastings, and the food she took was simple fare for the support of life, not for the gratification of appetite. She took her sleep for need, not for pleasure; and while the body rested, the mind watched, sometimes recalling things that she had read, sometimes continuing to think about the things of the day, planning how to finish what had been arranged or to prepare what was next to be done..."[1]

---

[1] St. Ambrose, *De Virginibus*, bk. 2, ch. 2.

PART III

MARY'S VIRTUES IN RELATION TO HERSELF

———

CHAPTER I

MARY'S JUSTICE

47. The virtues which are practiced towards men are subdivided into two groups, according as they have reference to others or to oneself. There is no intrinsic and essential difference between these two groups of virtues, for human nature is one in all men, and we ought to love it alike in ourselves and in others. There are, however, certain accidental differences with regard to the way in which these virtues are to be cultivated, and therefore it is that we are treating of them separately. All virtue in our relations with other men may be reduced to fraternal charity; but as regards oneself, one must acquire the virtue of *Justice*, which sanctifies the will; *Prudence*, which governs the rational faculty; *Temperance*, which curbs the movements of desire; *Fortitude*, which restrains the movements of anger.[1]   These

---

[1] *Quadruples enim invenitur subjectum huius virtutis (moralis) de qua nunc loquimur; scilicet rationale per essentiam, quod prudentia perficit, et rationale per participationem, quod dividitur in tria, id est, in voluntatem, quae est subjectum justitiae, et in concupiscibilem quae*

four are generally known as the Cardinal (or principal) Virtues, on which, as St. Gregory says, rests "the whole structure of our good work."[1]

Let us study these four virtues as they were found in Mary, and begin by speaking of her justice.

48. Justice, strictly speaking, consists in rendering everyone his due.[2] To every being we are bound to render that which belongs to it, namely the esteem and love which it truly deserves, neither more or less. The end must be regarded and loved as such, the means only as the means. The Creator is to be loved above all things, the creature only in its relation to the Creator. We may therefore give to the word justice a wider meaning. In this sense, justice is nothing less than sanctity itself or moral perfection;[3] and it is adorned

---

est subjectum temperantiae, et in irascibilem, quae est subjectum fortitudinis (St. Thomas *ST* I-II, q. 61, a. 2).

[1] *In quatuor virtutibus tota boni operis structura consurgit* (St. Gregory, *Moral*, II, ch. 49).

[2] *Virtus quae sua cuique tribuit* (St. Augustine, *De Civitate Dei*, ch. 12).

[3] *Justitia nihil aliud est quam omnium mandatorum custodia.* (St. John Chrystostom, Hom. 12, *in Matt.*)—*Servire autem*

with the resplendent aureola of one of the eight Beatitudes. "Blessed are they that hunger and thirst after justice, for they shall be filled."[1] It is in this highest sense of the word that we speak of Mary's justice.

49. To say that our Lady desired justice, is but little. She hungered and thirsted after justice, for she craved that food alone of which Jesus speaks, and which consists in doing the will of God,[2] she was a-thirst for that water which becomes to those that drink of it a "fount of water springing up unto life everlasting."[3] Her hunger and thirst were satiated with ineffable repletion, for she was *full of grace*.[4] Mary, filled with God's presence, pondered on His Law by day and by night, and as she meditated she was consumed with sweet yet ardent longings that God's name should be hallowed by all and in all, and that His will should be done on earth as in heaven. Assuredly no one ever sang with greater transport or better

---

Deo nihil aliud est quam bonis operibus tueri et conservare justitiam (Lactantius, *Div. Inst.*, bk. 3, ch. 9).

[1] Mt 5: 6.

[2] Jn 4: 34.

[3] Jn 4: 14.

[4] Lk 1: 28.

understood by experience than Mary did, the words of the Psalmist: "Blessed are they that search His testimonies, and that seek Him with their whole heart."[1]

50. But in Mary the virtue of justice not only attained to that sublime perfection which is common to other saints, who likewise hungered and thirsted after justice; but it passed beyond to such a height as was never reached or exceeded save by her Divine Son Jesus. We need hardly say that there was no taint of sin, original or actual, in her who was immaculate in the first moment of her conception.[2] But Mary was not merely free from all sin,[3] she was also adorned with such justice and holiness as befitted the Queen of all saints: *Regina sanctorum omnium.* This title with which we invoke our Lady day by day, implies that all the perfection of all the saints is found in her. As St. Peter Chrysologus says, grace was

---

[1] Ps 118: 1,2.

[2] *De qua (Virgine Maria) propter honorem Domini nullum prorsus, cum de peccatis agitur, haberi volo quaestionem* (St. Augustine, *De Natura et Gratia*, ch. 36).

[3] *Si quis dexerit hominem ... posse in tota vita peccata omnia, etiam venialia, vitare, nisi ex speciali Dei privilegio, quemadmodum de beata Virgine tenet Ecclesia, anathema sit* (Council of Trent, sess. 6, can. 23).

distributed among the saints in measure and degree, but upon Mary grace was poured forth in all its fullness.[1] The saints run their course with marvelous rapidity, so that their path is likened by the Wise Man to the light which gradually increases in splendor from dawn to perfect day.[2] If then we remember that Mary was full of grace from the very first instant of her existence and that she ever advanced from height to height, from virtue to virtue, we shall easily understand what an inestimable treasure of sanctity must have been amassed by her ere the close of her life.[3] Hence the Abbot Rupert said well of Mary that in her first moment of sanctification she was as the dawn, when she conceived her Divine Son she was like the moon, at her death she was like the sun.[4]

---

[1] *Singulis gratia se est largita per partes, Mariae vere simul se totam dedit gratiae plenitudo* (S. Peter Chrysologus, serm.143, *De Annunciatione*).

[2] *Justorum semita, quasi lux splendens, procedit et crescit usque ad perfectum diem* (Prv 4: 18).

[3] Segneri, *Il divoto di Maria*, ch. 3.

[4] *Eam in prima sanctificatione fuisse auroram, in Filii conceptione ut lunam, in morte ut solem.* (Rupert bk. 4 in Cant.).

ARTICLE I

MARY'S SIMPLICITY

51. Three most precious fruits of the virtue of Justice are simplicity, humility and gratitude. Simplicity is the sincere love of the pure and simple truth. Humility is the honest confession of one's own nothingness. Gratitude is the loving acknowledgment of benefits received. First let us consider our Blessed Lady's simplicity.

52. Once only is it recorded of our Lord in the Gospel that He expressed pleasure and satisfaction during His life on earth. It was when He rejoiced in spirit and gave thanks to His Father because the mysteries of God had been disclosed not to the wise and prudent, but to the little ones, such as are simple souls. "Jesus rejoiced in spirit and said, I thank Thee, O Father, Lord of heaven and earth that Thou hast hidden these things from the wise and prudent and hast revealed them unto little ones."[1] But who can say how often, while dwelling in the little cottage at Nazareth, He

---

[1] Lk 10: 21.

rejoiced in heart to see the child-like simplicity of His dear Mother, the guilelessness of mind and heart with which she worked and prayed, and the noble sincerity of her motives, of her deeds, of her words, of her silence? In that dear cottage at Nazareth all led a life of innocence and holiness. Their food was "the unleavened bread of sincerity and truth."[1] They cared and sought for God alone.[2] They spoke with the simple truthfulness of childhood: *Est, est; non, non.* Their speech was "yea, yea, nay, nay."[3] They thought and spoke well of all men, with loving dove-like simplicity.[4] Mary like Jesus with simple gaze saw God everywhere, in the birds of the air and in the lilies of the field, in men and in things.[5] She loved simplicity in everything, even in the practice of the highest virtues. She was simple in faith, believing in revealed truths without scrutiny; simple in hope, rejoicing in the happiness to come as though it were already present; simple in charity, for she loved only God or for God's sake. She was

---

[1] *In azymis sinceritatis et veritatis* (1 Cor 5: 8).

[2] *Unum necessarium* (Lk 10: 42).

[3] Mt 5: 37.

[4] *Estote simplices sicut columbae* (Mt 10: 16).

[5] *Oculus simplex* (Mt 6: 22).

simple in her thoughts, which were ever intent
on the Sun of Justice; in her judgments never
swayed by passion; in her affections virgin and
immaculate; in her words and deeds free from
duplicity and pretense. In fine, Mary in all
things showed herself simple as a dove.[1]

53. They say that genius is simple, because
it cares for but one thing, it lives for one idea
which absorbs all its energies. This is true of
the saints who, whether the world believes it
or not, are the greatest among men. In their
lives appears an admirable simplicity and
unity in thoughts, aims and affections. They
are governed by one idea, which seems to be
the polar star that directs their course. Their
one thought is of God, to whom they offer
their simple prayer: "One thing have I asked
of Thee, O my God, and this will I seek after,
that I may dwell in the house of my God all the
days of my life."[2] This simplicity of mind and
heart is compared in the language of Scripture
to keenness of sight. "When thine eye is

---

[1] *Simplicitatem columbae in omnibus repraesentans* (*Epist.
ad Paulam et Eustochium*, among the works dubiously
ascribed to St. Jerome, Migne edition).

[2] *Unam petii a Domino, hanc requiram, ut inhabitem in domo
Domini omnibus diebus vitae mene* (Ps 26: 4).

single," says our Lord, "thy whole body will be lightsome."[1] Hence our Lady is praised in the Canticle because her eyes are like those of the dove.[2] Indeed, Mary belonged wholly to her Beloved, as He was all hers. She had no other love in her heart than that of Jesus. "My Beloved to me and I to Him."[3] This explains the heroic intrepidity of Mary on Calvary. Weak and timid as she was, in that throng of soldiers, executioners and spectators who pressed around the cross, Mary, heedless of danger and forgetful of self, saw none but Jesus. Having followed Him to the foot of the cross, she mourned over Him and would have died with Him. Such was the simplicity of her love: *oculus simplex*.

---

[1] Lk 11: 34.

[2] *Oculi tui columbarum* (Cant. 1: 14).

[3] *Dilectus meus mihi et ego illi* (Cant. 2: 16).

ARTICLE II

MARY'S HUMILITY

54. True humility is justice to God and to ourselves. It is a deep sense of God's greatness and of our own nothingness. Hence St. Bernard in speaking of Mary's cardinal virtues, could find no more triumphant demonstration of her justice than that which is afforded by her humility. "The signal token of Mary's justice is her declaring herself to be the handmaid of the Lord."[1] Mary feels that she is nothing before God, who is all in all, and because she is the most humble she becomes the most highly exalted of all creatures, for the last must be first[2] and the lowly must be raised to high degree.[3]

55. But the perfection of humility does not consist in merely acknowledging one's own nothingness and vileness in comparison with God. It is more, it is to rejoice in one's own lowliness that all glory may be rendered to

---

[1] *Justitiae autem (Maria) praefert insigne, ubi se ancillam Domini confitetur* (St. Bernard, *De Diversis*, Serm. 52).

[2] *Sic erunt novissimi primi, et primi novissimi* (Mt 20: 16).

[3] *Qui se humiliat, exaltabitur* (Lk 14: 11).

Him who alone is great and worthy of honour. Now in the *Magnificat* we find the most humble Virgin taking ineffable complacency in her natural weakness and littleness. "He hath regarded the humility of His handmaid."[1] The Greek word here, rendered humility, really means lowliness. Mary's exultation is due to the fact that God has looked with favour upon her lowliness, that He has cast on her that glance of love and almighty power which raises the miserable from the dust and the poor out of the mire to set them among the princes of the people.[2] "He hath regarded the humility of His handmaid. Behold, henceforth all generations shall call me blessed."[3] O sublime humility, that brought God to live with men, that opened the gates of heaven to the exiles, that delivered our souls from the slavery of the demons! As the pride of the first man brought death to the world, so Mary's humility gave entrance to our life. Would that we too were humble, we who have so much to abase our pride! "If a man

---

[1] *Quia respexit humilitatem ancillae suae* (Lk 1: 48).

[2] Ps 112: 6–8.

[3] *Quia respexit humilitatem ancillae suae: ecce enim ex hoc beatam me dicent omnes generationes* (Lk 1: 48).

think himself to be something whereas he is nothing, he deceiveth himself."[1]

56. But we have other clear proofs of Mary's humility. She possessed in a special degree that generous instinct of self-effacement which characterizes humble souls. Their humility seeks to hide itself from the eyes of men, to avoid praise and honour, to bury itself in the obscurity of its own nothingness. Hence it was that Mary with mysterious silence concealed from Joseph the secret of her maternity, even when her spouse, a just man, could not but doubt her honour. Again, Mary, though purer than the angels, goes to be purified in the Temple as one unclean. She, the Mother of God, seems on Golgotha to be the mother of a criminal.

But yet more admirable is Mary's humility during the three years of Jesus' public life. She now conceals not merely her privileges but her very self. She seems forgotten by all, even by her Son. We do not find her amid the splendour of Thabor, nor in the wealthy and hospitable house of Lazarus at Bethany, nor at the

---

[1] *Nam si quis existimat se aliquid esse, cum nihil sit, ipse se seducit* (Gal 6: 3).

triumphal entry of Jesus into Jerusalem. Nay, on one occasion when she sought to speak with Jesus, He declined to see her, saying, "Who is My Mother and who are My brethren?" And stretching forth His hand towards His disciples, He said, "Behold My Mother and My brethren."[1] Lastly, after the glorious Ascension of our Lord, Mary lived in humility and obscurity, in subjection to St. John and the other apostles. Only after death was the most lowly Virgin to be exalted in proportion to her humility. She was delivered by the power of God from the ignominy of the grave and borne up into heaven and crowned as Queen of Angels.

————

ARTICLE III

MARY'S GRATITUDE

57.   Gratitude consists in the acknowledgement of benefits received and

---

[1] Mt 12: 48,49.

in the sense of being bound in love to the benefactor. This most attractive virtue is both a debt of justice and the effect of a loving humility which sees and loves in the benefactor the giver of the blessings it enjoys. Gratitude is commended to us by St. Paul: "Be ye thankful."[1] But unhappily it is rare among men, as we see from the judgment of the ten lepers cleansed by our Lord. One only of the ten returned to give thanks to the Divine Physician.[2] Let us then learn from Mary how to be grateful, since she is the model of every virtue.

58. The first and ordinary sign of gratitude is the giving of thanks. Expressions of thankfulness, when they are not mere cold words, but the manifestation of genuine feeling, reflect the likeness of a refined, humble and generous soul. Our whole life indeed ought to be one continuous act of thanksgiving to God inasmuch as it is but a series of divine gifts. "In all things give thanks, for this is the will of God in Christ Jesus concerning you all."[3] And yet we are forgetful and seldom think of the gifts

---

[1] *Grati estote* (Col 2: 15).

[2] Lk 17: 17.

[3] *In omnibus gratias agite: haec est enim voluntas Dei in Christo Jesu, in omnibus vobis* (1 Thes 5: 18).

which have come to us from above or of their Giver. Mary on the contrary was ever conscious of the infinite favours she had received from God, "Who had done great things to her."[1] She looked for the many, many gifts which God reserved for her in time to come, when "all nations should call her blessed."[2] Therefore, her whole life was spent in acts of thanksgiving and of love. They found their highest expression in the *Magnificat*, that marvelous hymn which surpasses in beauty and heavenly wisdom all the canticles of the prophets. Its sublime words could have been composed only by a soul full of unbounded and ineffable gratitude for the benefits bestowed on itself and all mankind, benefits which it regarded only as themes of praise to its merciful Benefactor.

59. But a grateful heart is shown, better than by words, by the good use of the gifts bestowed. On the other hand the wasting of the gift betrays an ungrateful mind. Now Mary, pure and sanctified from the first instant of her conception, was all her life long accumulating new treasures of sanctity. Thus she is a

---

[1] Lk 1: 49.

[2] Lk 1: 48.

luminous example of the gratitude with which the creature should employ the Creator's gift. Indeed our Blessed Lady, being full of grace from the outset and free from any incentive to sin, ascended without difficulty the path of virtue, passing from *strength to strength*. Nay, at every instant she doubled her treasure of grace. We know for certain that she was pure from all taint of sin and that she was always doing what was right, and therefore that she never left unused, even for one short hour, the precious talent that God every moment added to her store. Our Lady therefore doubled by her second act the merit of the first, and thus becoming richer in grace she doubled by a third act the merit of the second, and so on, till she amassed a treasure of sanctity such as created intelligence cannot conceive. I will not here go through the elaborate calculations attempted by some writers of this prodigious multiplication of grace during our Lady's long sojourn upon earth.[1] I will only add that Mary was praised by Jesus Christ Himself for her use of the gifts of God. He praised her publicly, not for being the Mother of God but for receiving lovingly every

---

[1] Signeri, *Il Divoto di Maria*, 1st part, ch. 3.

word or grace of God and making good use thereof. "Nay rather, blessed are they that hear the word of God and keep it."[1] These words of our Lord had special reference to Mary.

---

[1] Lk 11: 28.

VIRGO PRU-DENTISSIMA.

Eratque mulier illa prudentissima. 1. Reg. 25.

CHAPTER II

MARY'S PRUDENCE

60. The second of the Cardinal Virtues is
Prudence. While justice looks straight to the
end in view, prudence regards the choice of the
means which are useful or necessary for the
attainment of that end.[1] Prudence therefore is
a certain sagacity or keenness which enables

---

[1] *Ad prudentiam non pertinent praestituere finem virtutibus*

charity to discern what should be done or left undone, said or not said; to decide in fine, how every virtue may best be practiced according to the variety of times, places and persons.[1] The Holy Scriptures highly extol the prudence of Abigail, of Solomon and of the five wise virgins, and in a like manner we with Holy Church never weary of admiring the prudence of our Blessed Lady, whom we invoke every day with the glorious title of *Virgo prudentissima*.[2]

61. We have many luminous examples of our Lady's prudence. In her colloquy with Gabriel, when she enquired how the Divine Word would become incarnate within her, she was prudent, for we ought to ask for light from heaven to know not only what is to be done but how it must be done. In concealing from Joseph the mystery she bore in her womb, Mary was prudent, for it is good to leave to God the disclosure of things which only divine grace and not human reasonings can render credible.

---

moralibus, sed solum disponere de his quae sunt ad finem (St. Thomas, *ST* II-II, q. 47, a. 6).

[1] *Prudentia est amor, ea quibus adjuvatur, ab eis quibus impeditur, sagaciter eligens* (St. Augustine, *De Moribus Ecclesiae*, ch. 15).

[2] In the *Litany of Loreto*.

Again, Mary was prudent in quitting the house of Elizabeth before the birth of John the Baptist, in order to escape from the praise of men and to avoid the crowd of guests, for such diligent circumspection beseems a virgin. She was prudent in treasuring in her heart all the deeds and words of the Holy Child Jesus, for it was a thought of supernatural prudence to preserve those early and most precious incidents to which she alone could after time bear witness. She was prudent in her self-concealment during the days of Jesus' glory and again in appearing publicly on Golgotha when others fled, because it belongs to the prudence of charity to hinder by one's own example the scandal of the weak. Again Mary was prudent in not going with the other women to embalm the body of Jesus, because it was an act of rare prudence to testify to all her firm belief in the coming Resurrection while all others were weak in faith. In fine, Mary's prudence was to seek out and do in all things the most holy will of God, and this is the highest, the heavenly prudence, commended by St. Paul: "Become not unwise, but understanding what is the will of God."[1]

---

[1] Eph 5: 17.

62.   It is the special prerogative of prudence to aid others with good counsel, to dispel their ignorance, to remove their doubts, to show them the path they must follow, the perils they must avoid, and the precautions to be used.[1] Therefore we invoke the Virgin most prudent with the title of "Our Lady of Good Counsel." She is the Mother of Him who is the Counsellor,[2] and in the Divine Office those mysterious words are applied to Mary: "Counsel and equity are mine, prudence is mine."[3] Who is there among us that in time of temptation, of doubt, of perplexity, has invoked our dear Lady of Good Counsel, and has not obtained light, peace and ineffable joy? We all feel the truth and beauty of St. Bernard's words: "In dangers, in distress, in doubt, think of Mary, call on Mary's aid."[4]

---

[1] *Oportet quod ille sit praecipuus actus prudentiae, qui est praecipuus actus rationis agibilum; cujus quidem sunt tres actus. Quorum primus est consiliari* (St. Thomas, *ST* II-II, q. 47, a. 8).

[2] Is 9: 6.

[3] Prv 8: 14.

[4] St. Bernard, Hom. II, *Super Missus est*, circa finem.

ARTICLE I

MARY'S SILENCE

63. A great lesson taught us by prudence is to know when, where and how we should speak or be silent. Indeed, we are told by the Holy Ghost that he who knows how to govern his tongue, is most prudent. "He who refraineth his lips is wise."[1] It would be hard to say whether prudence appears to greater advantage in silence or in speech, for as vain loquacity and dull taciturnity are alike blameworthy, so one knows not whether to praise more highly in holy men their silence or their words. Anyhow, he is a perfect man who can fitly unite the prudence of silence with the prudence of speech. Such perfection is clearly seen in our Blessed Lady. Let us now begin to meditate upon her holy silence.

64. The Gospel mentions seven occasions only in which the Virgin Mother spoke. We are told but little of her early years prior to the angel's embassy, and not one word spoken by

---

[1] *Qui autem moderatur labia sua, prudentissimus est* (Prv 10: 19).

her during all those years is recorded. Then Joseph is a prey to cruel anguish on her account and is minded to put her away, but Mary is silent. At Bethlehem are heard the voices of the angels and of the shepherds, but Mary does not speak. During the flight into Egypt she is full of solicitude for her Child and intent on saving Him from His enemies, but she is silent. For the space of three years her Divine Son bears His good tidings from town to town and from village to village, while Mary communes with her own heart and keeps silent. Jesus speaks from His cross on Calvary, Mary is silent. The apostles receive in the guest chamber the gift of tongues, Mary is silent. These seven times of silence are full of eloquence to him who lovingly ponders on their mystery, and they may be arranged in the following order:—(1) *Silence of peace*, which conceals from the world Mary's early years, until she receives Gabriel's message. (2) *Silence of mystery*, namely, the secrecy which Mary observed concerning her divine conception, even with St. Joseph. (3) *Silence of meditation*, in which Mary gave birth to her Son and afterwards offered Him in the Temple to God for all mankind. (4) *Silence of humility*, during the time of exile in Egypt and afterwards in the humble home of Nazareth, where Mary lived as it were buried in concealment with her divine Son till the commencement of His Public Ministry. (5) *Silence of constancy*, in which Mary remained during the three years of her Son's preaching. (6) *Heroic silence*, with which she gazed on Jesus as He went on His way to Calvary, and again while she stood beneath the cross, and finally at His burial. (7) *Blissful silence*, in which she received with delight, but without making boast of them before men, the gifts and fruits of the Holy Ghost the Comforter on the day of Pentecost.

65. It has been said that silence is the language of angels, who communicate with one another without sound or words. Perhaps it is even better said that silence is the language of meditative souls who continually hold converse with God. God treats us, His creatures, with

great reverence.[1]   Therefore while we speak, He is silent. When we are still, He speaks and raises us to those supernatural thoughts and affections and heavenly colloquies which are granted only in solitude and silence.[2] Now she who had clothed with human nature the Substantial Word of God (*Verbum Patris*), assuredly did not care to divert herself with the talk of men, but loved to be silent, that she might converse in her heart with that Word, who when He no longer tarried in her womb remained in her soul. O how the voice of man must have grated on Mary's ear, accustomed as she was to the soft ineffable whisperings of the Word to her soul! How often she must have said within herself, "I will hearken to what the Lord God will say to me, for He will speak of peace."[3]

---

[1] *Tu autem dominator virtutis, cum tranquillitate judicas, et cum magna reverentia disponis nos* (Ws 12: 18).

[2] *Sedebit solitarius et tacebit, quia levavit super se* (Lam 3: 28).

[3] *Audiam quid loquetur in me Dominus Deus, quoniam loquetur pacem* (Ps 84: 9).

ARTICLE II

MARY'S WORDS

66. Prudence in the governing of the tongue appears not only in keeping silence, but also in the wise use of speech, for there is a time for everything, there is a time for speaking and a time for silence.[1] Now Mary spoke but little, and only seven words uttered by her are recorded in the Gospel; but when she did speak, all her words, like those of Jesus, were words of ineffable grace.[2]

67. On the subject of Mary's seven words, I cannot offer any comment more truthful or more devout than that which has been made on them by an author of our own time, who has thus written with his usual felicity of thought and language: "In Greek one and the same word signifies *to shine* and *to speak*, for the Greeks well knew that the word reveals the beauty of the soul, as the soul shows forth the glory of God. Ah, said I to myself, truly Mary's seven

---

[1] *Tempus tacendi et tempus loquendi* (Eccles. 3: 7).

[2] *Et omnes...mirabantur in verbis gratiae, quae procedebant de ore ipsius* (Lk 4: 22).

words are so many rays of light from the purest and noblest soul that ever was or will be, save Jesus Christ alone. They are like the seven beauteous rays and colours of the rainbow, God's token of peace to men. What joy, ever the same and yet ever new, descends upon the soul from each of those words! The first of them is the maiden's question to a heavenly messenger: 'How shall this be done, because I know not man?' (Lk 1: 34). The second is her humble consent to become the Mother of God: 'Behold the handmaid of the Lord, be it done to me according to thy word.' (Lk 1: 38). The third is a joyous greeting addressed to an aged relative who has become a mother by a heavenly prodigy: 'Mary entered into the house of Zachary and saluted Elizabeth' (Lk 1: 40). The fourth word immediately follows and is an inspired canticle: 'My soul doth magnify the Lord.' (Lk 1: 46). The fifth breathes a mother's lament or perhaps a mother's fear for the loss of her child: 'Son, why hast Thou done so to us? Behold Thy father and I have sought Thee sorrowing.' (Lk 2: 48). The sixth is the petition which Mary's kind heart offered to Jesus at the marriage-feast, to spare the confusion of the newly-wedded pair: 'They have no wine' (Jn 2: 3). Finally, the seventh word, which was spoken at the same feast, contains the commandment of Christian perfection: 'Whatsoever He shall say to you, do ye' (Jn 2: 5)."[1]

68. In order that our words may not be idle, they must be pleasing to God, meritorious in the speaker and edifying to the listener. Such were Mary's seven words. The first was an utterance of *virgin purity*, the second of *humble obedience*, the third of *reverence* and *modesty*, the fourth of *grateful exultation*, the fifth of *authority* and *mildness*, the sixth of *tender charity*, the seventh of *unwavering faith*. Thus all the words of Mary were acts of lofty virtue, such as befitted her who was to offer us an example of all the virtues. Would that we could follow her even afar off, for "he who offends not in his words, is a perfect man."[2]

---

[1] Paolo Perez, *I sette silenzi e le sette parole di Maria*, Introduction.

[2] *Si quis in verbo non offendit, hic perfectus est vir* (Jas 3: 2).

CHAPTER III

MARY'S TEMPERANCE

69. Another of the Cardinal Virtues is Temperance, which restrains the inordinate cravings of the faculty of desire.[1] In truth, the Immaculate Virgin had no inordinate cravings, but only well-ordered instincts which drew her to the true, the good and the beautiful in all things. Hence, when we would discourse on Mary's temperance, we can only speak of her moderation in the use of external things, that is, her poverty, and of her self-control in

---

[1] St. Thomas, *ST* II-II, q. 141, a. 2.—St. Ambrose in enumerating the cardinal virtues makes mention of temperance in the first place: *Scimus virtutes esse quatuor cardinales, temperantiam, justitiam, prudentiam, fortitudinem* (*In Lucam*, ch. 6). St. Thomas, however, (*ST* I-II, q. 61, a. 2) gives temperance the third place among the cardinal virtues, as we have also done, though elsewhere (*ST* II-II, q. 141) he treats of temperance last after the other three.

the use of lawful pleasures, that is, her virgin chastity. But first we must raise our thoughts to another kind of temperance more sublime, nay, heavenly, which regards even the supernatural delights of the soul. In truth, the supernatural order has its secret and ineffable pleasures, which are tasted by the pure of heart, and are a foretaste of the uncreated beauty and goodness, God Himself. Hence the consolations, the ecstasies of love, the ravishment of mind, which the saints have sometimes experienced, lost as it were in an ocean of heavenly delights. But earth is not our home, and while we dwell in this vale of tears, oftentimes it behooves us to forego these ineffable delights. This is precisely what is required by that temperateness of rarest excellence which, as we have said, regards the supernatural joys of the soul. Simon Peter seems to have lacked this spiritual temperateness when he could not bear to lose the heavenly delights of Thabor, and cried out in his eagerness:—"Lord, it is good for us to be here."[1] On the other hand the imagination cannot picture one more temperate in the

---

[1] *Domine, bonum est nos hic esse: si vis, faciamus hic tria tabernacula* (Mt 17: 4).

enjoyment of divine things than Mary who was ever tranquil and self-possessed, alike in the unspeakable joy of her Child's birth, and in the unspeakable sorrow of Golgotha.

70. Who ever experienced upon earth joy so great and so holy as Mary's was when at Bethlehem she saw that she was the Mother of God made man, and when at Nazareth she watched the Divine Child in His daily life, and called Him by that sweet name, "My Son," a name which till then none but His Heavenly Father had given Him?[1] But in the midst of this divine joy Mary's soul was never, as far as we know, rapt in ecstasy or bereft of bodily sense. She checked the course of those joyous affections, and restrained them in her profound peace of soul, a glimpse of which escaped, like a ray of tranquil light, in the smile on her lips and in the virgin candor that showed itself in her looks and bearing. But what shall we say of the self-command which Mary exhibited in the time of sorrow? We all know how often the sword of grief pierced the heart of the Virgin Mother, but it never wounded her so cruelly as it did on Calvary, when she stood by the cross

---

[1] *Filius meus es tu* (Ps 2: 7).

of her Son. Other women in her plight would have shown their anguish by wild words of lament and wild gestures. Mary, composed, modestly clad in the garb of mourning, her heart full of faith, hope and love as her eyes were of tears, stood erect by her Son's cross in silent adoration.[1] Christians, who while you are still novices in the spiritual life, are querulous with God because He sometimes denies you the milk and honey of His consolations, learn to be temperate even in spiritual pleasures. Be like Mary, equally ready for things bitter and things sweet in the service of God, and say with the psalmist, *My heart, O God, is ready* for all things, *I will sing hymns and psalms* of thanksgiving and praise.[2]

---

[1] *Stabat verecunda, modesta, lacrimis plena, doloribus immersa* (St. Antonine, *Summa Theologica Moralis,* part 4, 15, ch. 41, §1).

[2] *Paratum cor meum, Deus, paratum cor meum: cantabo et psalmum dicam* (Ps 56: 8).

MATER CASTISSIMA.

Flores simul

et Fructus.

O quàm pulchra est casta generatio? *Sap.*

ARTICLE I

MARY'S POVERTY

71.   The virtue of temperance is fitly accompanied by the kindred virtues of voluntary *poverty* and virgin *chastity*, whereby the soul loses all love for earthly substance

and pleasures. Let us say something of Mary's poverty.

72. Mary, though she came of the ancient line of David and of Solomon, was born of Joachim and Anna at a time when the royal house had been brought to poverty. She was espoused to a poor artisan of Nazareth, and as long as she lived, she was poor. But her poverty was not merely the condition of life in which her lot was cast: it was also a virtue loved and practiced by free choice. Nay, according to some writers, she generously bound herself thereto by vow.[1] Mary indeed possessed in God the abundance of all good and had no need of anything beyond. Hence she gloried in possessing nothing else than God and magnified Him for His bounty to the poor. "He hath filled the hungry with good things, and the rich He hath sent empty away."[2] Moreover, the great love she bore to Jesus, who being infinitely rich made Himself poor for our sake,[3] could not fail to enamour her of poverty as a thing desirable and delightful, according to the

---

[1] St. Alphonsus, *Glories of Mary*, part II, §7.

[2] *Esurientes implevit bonis, et divites dimisit inanes* (Lk 1: 53).

[3] 2 Cor 8: 9.

words of Jesus: "Blessed are the poor in spirit, for theirs is the kingdom of heaven."[1]

73. But Mary's poverty, though voluntary and most honourable, was not exempt from unspeakable humiliations and sorrows. At a time when God still rewarded virtue with the fatness of the earth and the dews of heaven, and in a nation which remembered as its saints of old, men who had been rich and powerful—poverty, like sterility, must have seemed a curse from heaven, and must have brought with it ignominy as well as suffering. We need not dilate on all that the Virgin Mother must have suffered in her poverty. Nazareth, Bethlehem and Egypt can tell us what the humble roof, scanty fare and bitter exile must have been for the daughter of the kings of Judah. It is true that the love of Jesus gladdened her amid all her pains. But on the other hand, there are moments in which one who is poor, even though he be so by choice, feels most keenly his penury: for instance when he receives some noble guest whom he reveres and loves, but to whom he cannot offer fitting hospitality. Then

---

[1] *Beati pauperes spiritu, quoniam ipsorum est regnum coelorum* (Mt 5: 3).

indeed he laments his poverty and cannot find words to excuse his inability to do honour to his guest. How often must the Virgin Mother have shared these wounded feelings of the poor! In her poverty she must shelter and support for nearly thirty years the Son of God. When He was newly-born she could only give Him a bed of hay. His lodging was a stable, and His cradle a manger. Afterwards she saw Him dwelling in an obscure village, unhonoured, unnoticed, laboring in a humble workshop. Next she must allow Him to be maintained by poor women who followed Him and supplied Him with His daily food. Finally, she had not even a tomb in which to lay Him, but must be beholden to another for the resting-place of her Son. How often in these straights her maternal heart must have been rent with anguish, and how often she must have felt the deep void of her poverty! The world is wont to regard wealth with envy and esteem, and it knows nothing of the hidden loveliness of voluntary poverty. But this treasure is appreciated by the saints. Voluntary poverty, ever since Jesus and Mary made it known and glorified by their example, has been the wealth of generous souls and the nourishment of virtues.

ARTICLE II

MARY'S VIRGIN CHASTITY

74. Virginity, the crowning perfection of chastity, is a virtue angelic rather than human. There never was and never will be an example of this virtue equal to that of our dear Lady, insomuch that *Mary* and *Blessed Virgin* are regarded as words synonymous.[1]

75. Mary was the first to plant the lily of this most delicate virtue in the garden of the Church. St. Ambrose calls her the standard-bearer of virginity, for she first unfurled its banner.[2] It is true that Rome had its Vestal Virgins, but not only was it difficult to find six or seven maidens for the service of Vesta, but moreover their virginity was ostentatious and lasted only for a time. It was not life-long, humble and modest. The virgin-daughter of Jefte[3] too

---

[1] *Quis unquam aut quo saeculo proferre ausus est nomen sanctae Mariae, et interrogatus non statim intulit Virginis nomen? Non altera videtur sanctae Mariae vox et virgo* (St. Epipanius, *Haeres.* 78).

[2] *Quae signum sacras virginitatis extulit* (St. Ambrose, *De Instit. Virg.*, ch. 5).

[3] Jgs 11.

was celebrated in the history of the Hebrews, but hers was but a piteous case of enforced virginity. Mary was the first who when there was no precept, no counsel, no precedent for a perpetual vow of virginity, consecrated from her childhood the flower of her maidenhood by vow to God.[1] A most ancient tradition (of which we find a trace in the very Koran of Mahomet) affirms that Mary when she was perhaps only three years old, was presented in the Temple of Jerusalem, and that there she vowed to God the stainless lily of her purity. This tradition has given occasion to a festival kept in the Eastern Church from the 12th century and celebrated by the Latin Church on the 21st of November. At any rate, whatever may be believed regarding the exact time at which Mary pronounced her vow, it certainly was before the Annunciation. Otherwise, as St. Augustine observes,[2] there would be no meaning in her words to the angel:

---

[1] *Illud vere certum est ex sacra Scriptura, de nullo alio colligi posse, ante Virginem hoc votum (virginitatis) emisisse* (Suarez, *De Mysteriis Christi*, q. 28, disp. 6, sect. 3).

[2] *Quomodo, inquit, fiet istud, quoniam virum non cognosco? Quod profecto non diceret, nisi Deo virginem se antea vovisset* (St. Augustine, *De Sancta Virginitate*, ch. 4).

"How shall this be done, because I know not man?"[1]

76.   The words *Quomodo fiet istud quoniam virum non cognosco,* not only reveal the promise which Mary had made in her heart, but also clearly indicate that she would actually have foregone divine maternity rather than her maidenhood, for there is no state so exalted that virginity is not higher.[2] The angel's words of praise troubled Mary's humility—*turba est in sermone ejus*—but did not alarm her. When she hears of the Son that is to be born of her, she is alarmed and enquires of the angel: "How shall this be done, because I know not man?" This is the holy and humble dignity

---

[1] Lk 1: 34.

[2] Together with many other Fathers of the Church St. Augustine notes that maternity as such, even if divine, is less perfect and pleasing to God than a chaste virginity professed and accepted in a spirit of charity, i.e., in the words of Jesus, "for the sake of the Kingdom of Heaven" (cf. Mt 19:12, also Catechism of the Catholic Church, § 1618-20). Hence, in view of her vow, Mary asked how she could substitute the lesser good for the higher in offering herself to God. The Angel's reply resolved the dilemma: it would be precisely the conservation of Mary's perpetual virginity which would make possible the divine Maternity and hence would involve no substitution. Our Lord makes the same point in Lk 11: 27–28. [Editor's note.]

of virginity.[1] Hence it is that the Holy Fathers when they praise the virginity of Mary can find no imagery fully equal to the expression of their thought. They call her the "Garden Enclosed," the "Fountain Sealed Up," the "Eastern Gate," and give her other titles without end. Also the faithful generally, with their unerring supernatural instinct, not finding words apt to describe our Lady's virgin purity, speak of her as "most chaste," "without stain," "Virgin of virgins," "most pure," "inviolate," "without equal," *Virgo singularis*.

77. She is indeed *Virgo singularis*, for she is Virgin and Mother. This marvelous combination of maidenhood with maternity accorded well with the dignity of the Son of God, who should be born *natura mirante*, to the amazement of nature. Likewise it befitted the dignity of God's own Mother who should bring forth her Son with mysterious childbirth, *partu admirando*.[2] It was the prodigy foretold more than seven hundred years previously: "Behold

---

[1]   *Vergine pura, d'ogni parte intera,*
      Vergine sola al mondo, senza esempio,
      Cui nè prima fu simil nè seconda.
      (Petrarch, Canz. 8).

[2] *Deum hujusmodi decebat nativitas, qua nonnisi de Virgine*

a virgin shall conceive and bear a Son, and His
name shall be called Emmanuel."[1]

———

ARTICLE III

MARY'S MODESTY

78. The cardinal virtue of temperance—to
which appertain voluntary poverty and virgin
chastity—should not be disjoined from the fair
virtue of modesty. Modesty and temperance
are, indeed, two aspects of one and the same
virtue,[2] which is named temperance insofar as
it controls the interior movements of the mind
and will, and modesty insofar as it directs the

---

*nasceretur. Talis congruebat et Virgini partus, ut non pareret
nisi Deum* (St. Bernard, Homil. 2, *Super Missus est*).

[1] Is 7: 14.

[2] *Modestia utique dicta est a modo, et a temperie temperantia.
Ubi autem modus est atque temperies, nec plus est quidquam
nec minus* (St. Augustine, *De Beata Vita*, ch. 4, n. 32).

actions and deportment of the outer man. To each of these forms of virtue may be applied the adage of the ancients: *Ne quid nimis*.

79. St. Ambrose and St. Bernard[1] were enamoured of Mary's modesty which seemed to them the perfect exemplar of this virtue. Doubtless, that which ravaged the soul of Denis the Areopagite when he beheld the Mother of God, was her modesty which reflected as in a mirror all the God-like ways of Jesus. Ever quick to imitate all that was good and beautiful, she had under her eyes for so many years the Divine Type of modesty, Jesus Christ.[2] Love led her to copy His graciousness and refinement. For my part I cannot picture Mary to myself except as tranquil in her look, tender in her smile, attentive in listening, discreet in replying, ever neat in dress, dignified in action, courteous of manner, erect without haughtiness, prudent in speech. She wept without bitterness or agitation. There was no boldness, no curiosity in her looks. All this and much more

---

[1] *Si Mariam diligitis, si contenditis ei placere, aemulamini modestiam ejus* (St. Bernard, serm. *in Dom. Infra Octav. Assumpt. B.V.*, n. 2)—cf. St. Ambrose, *De Virgin.*, bk. II. *post initium.*

[2] 2 Cor 10: 1.

the greatest artists have striven to depict, but never with full success.

80. Modesty befits us all, but especially it is the requisite for woman, if she is to be that pure being, filled with the fear of God, that is praised, by the Holy Ghost.[1] Hence it was needful that Mary, the type of perfect womanhood, should give us many an example of admirable modesty. A rare example of modesty is Mary's silence when, reluctant through delicacy to disclose to anyone the glory of her divine maternity, she concealed even from Joseph the Mystery she bore in her womb. Again, the quiet words *they have no wine,* with which she made her request to Jesus at the marriage-feast, reveal the modest and delicate reserve with which the loving Mother treats her Almighty Son. Again, the gentle enquiry she addressed to Jesus on finding Him in the Temple, "Son why hast Thou done so to us?"[2] breathes the modesty of a mother's fears rather than a mother's lament. In fine, Mary is the constant and resplendent image of Him whose voice was so kind and subdued that it never grew harsh or loud, and

---

[1] *Fallax gratia et vana est pulchritudo: mulier timens Dominum ipsa laudabitur* (Prv 31: 30).

[2] Lk 2: 48.

who was so considerate and so mild that He would not break a bruised reed or quench the smoking flax. [1]

---

[1] *Non contendet, neque clamabit, neque audiet aliquis in plateis vocem ejus: arundinem quassatam non confringet et linum fumigans non extinguet* (Mt 12: 19,20).

CHAPTER IV

MARY'S FORTITUDE

81.   One of Mary's cardinal virtues yet remains for our consideration. It is her fortitude. Assuredly hers was not the fortitude of the Jewish heroines, of Deborah who led the soldiers of Israel, of Jael who killed Sisara, of Judith who smote Holofernes. No, but Mary had that nobler, more generous fortitude which consists in the mastery of self, and of which we are told by the Holy Ghost that "he who ruleth his spirit is better than he who taketh cities."[1]   While justice presses toward the *end* in view, and prudence chooses the *means*, and temperance regulates the use to be made of these same means, fortitude finally is that

---

[1] *Qui dominator animo suo (melior) expugnatore urbium* (Prv 16: 32).

indomitable virtue which surmounts all the obstacles that beset the use of the means and the attainment of the end. Hence it is fortitude which must render a man superior to his natural weakness, master of himself and of his passionate instincts, to the end that he may do and endure great things and fight valiantly in the warfare of the spirit. "Resist ye strong in faith."[1]

82. It is a grievous error to imagine that Mary's life was one of quiet repose and tranquil contemplation, whereas in reality she was continually being put to the proof by sorrow and by unspeakable sufferings which were all the greater because they were interior, secret, known to God alone and worthy of a magnanimous soul. The poverty of the crib, the flight into Egypt, the sword of Simeon's prophecy, contempt from the Nazarenes, persecution from the Jews, and finally Gethsemani, the Praetorium, Calvary, all these show us as it were the tissue of Mary's life. It was a life of martyrdom. The unchanging calmness with which she bravely sustained afflictions, so many and so grievous,

---

[1] *Resistite fortes in fide* (1 Pet 5: 9).

is the proof of her complete self-command. Mary felt sorrow keenly, but her sorrow was heightened by entire conformity to God's holy will. Though she was free from the incentive to sin,[1] she had the passions essential to human nature, but they were subject to her will and were all pervaded by the dominant passion of the saints, which is the love of God. Hence the Holy Fathers have deemed Mary to be prefigured by the valiant woman described in Holy Writ—a type of womanhood rarely found, or rather, found in Mary alone.[2]

83. That marvellous law of God's action whereby He chooses the weak to confound the strong,[3] was never so brilliantly displayed as in Mary. To this lowly maiden of Nazareth God gave the strength and might of that supernatural fortitude which comes of faith, of humility and of love, three forms of virtue of a higher order than even the cardinal virtue of fortitude. Indeed, love is a force which gently subdues and softens men's hearts, binds them with its fetters and makes them amenable to all it

---

[1] Suarez, *De Mysteriis Christi*, q. 27, a. 6, disp. 4, sect. 5, n. 2.

[2] *Procul et de ultimis finibus pretium ejus* (Prv 31: 10).

[3] *Infirma mundi elegit Deus, ut confundat fortia* (1 Cor 1: 27).

wills. Now the saints who have studied most deeply the virtues of Mary, have found in her love for Jesus the secret of that power whereby she asks rather as queen than as handmaid.[1] Faith likewise is a force strong enough to move mountains.[2] Did not Mary by this power of her faith hasten the time of the Redeemer's miracles, and afterwards become his wonderworker of all ages, so that St. Peter Damian has ventured to apply to her those words: "All power is given to thee on heaven and on earth"?[3] Lastly, humility is that irresistible force which overthrows the "father of pride," the "old adversary," whose head was crushed by Mary's foot, that is, by her lowliness.[4] Thus she became to him terrible as an army ready for battle.[5]

---

[1] *Non solum rogans, sed imperans: domina, non ancilla* (St. Peter Damian, Serm. 1, *De Nativ. B. V.*).

[2] Mt 17: 19.

[3] *Data est tibi omnis potestas in caelo et in terra* (St. Peter Damian, Serm. 1, *De Nativ. B. V.*).

[4] *Ipsa conteret caput tuum et tu insidiaberis calcaneo ejus* (Gen. 3: 15).

[5] *Terribilis ut castrorum acies ordinata* (Cant. 6: 3).

ARTICLE I

MARY'S MAGNANIMITY

84. From fortitude, as St. Thomas Aquinas tells us,[1] are derived the generous virtues of magnanimity, patience and perseverance. The first is fortitude in performing great and noble deeds.[2] The second is fortitude in the endurance of evil.[3] The third is fortitude in well-doing and in long-suffering unto the end.[4] Perhaps the counsel of the Psalmist refers to these three virtues: "Do manfully and let thy heart take courage and wait thou for the Lord."[5]

85. As I pause to think of Mary's magnanimity, I ask myself: Who, after Jesus had as great a soul as the Virgin Mother? She

---

[1] St. Thomas, *ST* II-II, q. 129–137.

[2] *Magnanimitas ex suo nomine importat quondam extensionem animi ad magna* (St. Thomas, *ST* II-II, q. 129, a. 1).

[3] *Potentia aequo animo mala toleramus* (St. Augustine, *De Patientia*, ch. 2).

[4] *Sustinere difficultatem quae provenit ex diurnitate boni operis, dat laudem perseverantiae* (St. Thomas, *ST* II-II, q. 137, a. 2).

[5] *Viriliter age, et confortetur cor tuum, et sustine Dominum* (Ps 26: 14).

was full of grace, and therefore full of God: *gratia plena.* But God is great, and as He cannot dwell in a heart that is mean and narrow, He enlarges the hearts which He chooses for His abode, and this He does in proportion to the measure in which He wills to impart Himself. "I ran the way of Thy commandments when Thou didst enlarge my heart."[1] Therefore God, who has bestowed more and better gifts on Mary than on any other of His creatures, must have also given her a soul great beyond conception, a soul capable of receiving those graces of the Holy Ghost which were at every moment poured out upon her in superabundance. In fine, Mary must have been capable of all those great and mysterious things which the Almighty alone can effect in the soul. "He that is mighty hath done great things to me."[2]

86. Mary's magnanimity may be still better appreciated by recalling to mind what has already been said of the boundless love she bore for the human race: magnanimous love which made her our co-redemptrix.[3] Jesus

---

[1] *Viam mandatorum tuorum cucurri, cum dilatasti cor meum* (Ps 118: 32).

[2] *Fecit mihi magna qui potens est* (Lk 1: 49).

[3] *Adjutorium Redemptionis* (Albertus Magnus *super Missus*

Christ alone is our Redeemer, but it was Mary who conceived Him in her womb and gave Him to the world. She nourished the Divine Infant at her breast, cherishing Him lovingly, guarding Him with a mother's care. Finally, she accompanied Him to Golgotha, and with heart-rending anguish but with firm resolve she offered Him to His Father as a holocaust for peace and redemption. Therefore in very truth she co-operated in the redemption of mankind. Assuredly it was profound wisdom which ordained that Mary should emerge from the obscurity in which she had been concealed for nearly three years and should be seen on Calvary at the foot of the cross. All will readily admit that Mary had a kind of claim on that life of Jesus which she herself had given Him. It was therefore just that she should be present on the hill of Calvary to manifest in the sight of Heaven and earth her consent to her Son's sacrifice. This she did by her patient grief, uniting the heroism of the Mother to the heroism of the Son.

est, ch. 53).

ARTICLE II

MARY'S PATIENCE

87. Fortitude of soul is shown not only by magnanimity, but also even more by patience, for, as we have said, the cardinal virtue of fortitude consists in self-mastery, a thing which we can only obtain by patience. "In patience ye shall possess your souls."[1] Now, as St. James tells us, patience is the crowning perfection of all virtues, *opus perfectum*,[2] for a virtue reaches its highest excellence through the meek endurance of pain, that is, by patience.[3]

After Jesus Christ, the most perfect exemplar of patience is His Virgin Mother.

88. First of all, we must reflect that our Lady's life was one uninterrupted exercise of sublime patience. Indeed, we shall never think ourselves capable of appreciating it, if we consider that the true country of an Immaculate Virgin must be the Eden of innocence, whereas it behooved Mary to dwell, like us, in this vale

---

[1] *In patientia vestra possidebitis animas vestras* (Lk 21: 19).

[2] *Patientia autem opus perfectum habet* (Jas 1: 4).

[3] St. Augustine, *De Patientia*, ch. 2.

of tears, in this land of sin. Who can describe the mysterious and painful conflict in thoughts and affections and deeds between that creature of innocence and sinful men like ourselves? As some exotic plant that in a foreign clime and in the midst of wild vegetation grows and thrives in spite of excessive cold or heat and unsuitable nourishment and the violence of the winds; even so the Immaculate Virgin, the flower of paradise, was fain to live like any other daughter of Eve in a world made not for her but for the heirs of sin and pain. She, though sinless, must endure misery and death, the inheritance of sin. She could not enter into the world's way of thinking, of loving and acting, while the world could not understand her heavenly mode of life. The heat of day was too scorching for this flower of Eden. The herbs and fruits of earth were too bitter for her whose country was heaven. I cannot find words that fully express my meaning, but this is always the thought which predominates in my mind and heart when I meditate on the mystery of Mary's Immaculate Conception. This mystery, it seems to me, does not cease with the first moment of Mary's life but lasts all her life long. It is the mystery of the unfailing patience shown by a sinless daughter of heaven who for seventy years was constrained to dwell among us, children of sin, and be an exile with us in sorrow and in pain.

89. There was an hour in Mary's life when her patience was unbounded and earned for her the aureola of Queen of Martyrs. It was when she stood by the cross of Jesus. If the heroism of patience consists in enduring great sorrow with great dignity and peace of soul, then surely this heroism shines forth in the example of the Virgin Mother on Calvary. Consider the abyss of sorrow into which that soul is plunged, and yet she is in peace. Sadness beyond words appears in her countenance, and but too clearly betokens the sharp sword which is piercing her soul and spirit. But her quiet dignity and her silence as she stands erect near the cross, reveal the calmness of her sorrow. The Evangelist, as St. Ambrose remarks, makes no mention of our Lady's tears but shows her to us as she stands almost motionless beneath the cross. "I read that she stood, I read not that she wept."[1]

---

[1] *Stantem lego, flentem non lego* (St. Ambrose, *De Instit.*

Perhaps the reason is that the Gospel would have us think not so much of the greatness of Mary's sorrow as the admirable heroism of her patience. Certainly we need not wonder that the Mother of Sorrows wept beneath the cross, *juxta crucem lacrimosa*, for what mother would not weep over the agony of her son? But truly marvelous is the peace and restfulness with which Mary sanctifies her tears and sustains her immense affliction. We know that Abraham ascended the mountain to immolate his son, but the mother did not go to see the knife made ready to slay the child of promise. Here on Golgotha it is the mother herself who generously offers an Infinite Victim, whose blood *speaketh better than the blood of Abel*.[1] Agar was faithful to her outcast child, but she could not bear to see him die.[2] Mary on the contrary stands on the summit of Golgotha and gazes on the Crucified. Her anguish is unutterable, and yet she is surrounded by an atmosphere of peace. *O Queen of martyrs!*

Virgin., ch. 7 and *De Obitu Valentiniani Consolatio*).

[1] Heb 12: 24.

[2] *Non videbo morientem puerum* (Gen. 21: 16).

ARTICLE III

MARY'S PERSEVERANCE

90. Fortitude, as we have said, produces also the virtue of perseverance.[1] We do not here refer to final perseverance, which consists in dying a holy death, and which is not a virtue, but a "great gift of God," as the Council of Trent has declared.[2] Indeed, everyone is aware, that Mary's gift of final perseverance was not only unusual, but without example, for she did but pass from an ecstasy of divine love into the sweet slumber of death in the Lord.[3] But the perseverance of which we must now speak is that manly virtue whereby the just continue to do what is right, with long-suffering and constancy, without swerving to the right or to the left. Now who or what could ever have turned aside the Immaculate Mother of God from seeking the highest good? Without doubt

---

[1] *Perseverantia adjungitur fortitudini sicut virtus secondaria principali* (St. Thomas, *ST* II-II, q. 137, a. 2).

[2] *Magnam perseverantiae donum* (Council of Trent Sess. 6 Can. 16).

[3] *Fulcite me floribus, stipate me malis, quia amore langueo* (Cant. 2: 5).

she could say with firmest assurance: "Neither death, nor life, nor angels, nor principalities, nor powers, nor things present, nor things to come, nor might, nor height, nor depth, nor any other creature shall be able to separate me from the love of God, which is in Christ Jesus our Lord."[1] Hence Christian theology maintains that Mary was "confirmed in grace,"[2] and that she remained ever holy and pure from the least taint of sin.[3]

91.   But there is another characteristic peculiar to our Lady's virtue of perseverance. Not only did she persevere in holiness, but she continually from the beginning to the end of her life increased in sanctity and in grace, rising from strength to strength, from virtue to virtue. It is true that Mary was always full of God's presence, and devoid of any other love than His;[4] but when grace fills men's souls with God, it increases their capacity and again fills them to the full.[5] The work of grace is to replenish the

---

[1] Rom 8: 38,39.

[2] Suarez, *De Mysteriis Christi*, disp. 4, sect. 4.

[3] *Tota pulchra* (Cant. 4: 7).

[4] *Gratia plena* (Lk 1: 28).

[5] *Ipsa anima, quantum plus recipit de bonitate divina et lumine gratiae ipsius, tanto   capacior efficitur ad recipiendum*

soul that is ready to receive it, and to inundate the soul that is full, whereas the work of sin is to leave the soul devoid of all good. Hence St. Augustine has aptly said of Mary that she was *filled with grace*, and of Eve that she was *made destitute by sin*.[1] This will help us to understand how Mary's soul inundated by grace ever stayed its progress in sanctity. A noble river, whose waters flow ever onwards, with those of many tributaries till they are lost in the ocean, is an image of Mary, who continually advanced, growing from fullness to fullness, immaculate in her conception, holy in her life, and finally Queen of the saints in heaven. Also the dawn, pale at first, which clothes itself with light that grows more vivid every moment, till at length it reaches the splendour of full mid-day, is an image of Mary, who from the earliest day-break of life increased the heat and light of her virtues even to that noonday which knows no sunset, the noonday of eternal glory. "She cometh forth as the morning rising."[2]

---

et ideo quanto plus recipit, tanto plus potest recipere (St. Thomas, *Super Sent.*, b. 1, d. 17, q. 2, a. 4, co.).

[1] *Maria impleta est gratia et Eva vacuata est a culpa* (Serm. 17, *de Sanctis,* attributed to St. Augustine).

[2] *Progreditur quasi aurora consurgens* (Cant. 6: 9).

CONCLUSION

———

92. Meditation on the virtues of the Mother of God leads us of necessity to infer that Mary is an exemplar of perfect sanctity, and that whereas other saints have reflected rays of the beauty of holiness, in her there was resplendent completeness of virtue and beauty. Like rays of light gathered into a focus, all the virtues of the saints are concentrated in Mary.[1] Hence Christian nations are constrained by force of reasoning to admire and extol more and more from age to age the "Blessed among women." Hence the Greeks call her *Panagia*, that is, all-holy, and the Latins say that she is "beyond all praise"[2] while none can find one holier or higher than Mary, after God and His Christ.[3]

---

[1] *Ipsa etiam omnium virtutum opera exercuit, alii autem sancti specialia quaedam; quia alius fuit humilis, alius castus, alius misericors, et ideo ipsi dantur in exemplum virtutum... Sed B. Virgo in exemplum omnium virtutum* (St. Thomas. *In Expositione in Salutationem Angelicam*).

[2] *Quibus te laudibus efferam, nescio* (Office of the Blessed Virgin).

[3] *Qua major sub Deo nullatenus intelligitur* (Pius IX, *in bulla "Ineffabilis Deus"*).

93. But is a mere barren admiration of Mary's holiness to be the only fruit of these our meditations? Ah, Mary should be the object not simply of admiration but also of imitation. Created as we are to the image and likeness of God, we ought to regard God Himself as our Exemplar of Holiness; but to imitate His infinite sanctity seemed impossible to fallen man. Therefore God in His ineffable mercy gave us for our model His own Son Incarnate, Jesus Christ. But even the virtues of Jesus are those of a God-man. It was fitting, therefore, that the Divine Goodness should offer us yet another model, which should be nearer to ourselves, and which all might more easily copy. Now this model was given us in her who is the most perfect image of Jesus Christ, even as He is the perfect image of God. Wherefore it seems to me that the Blessed Virgin, resplendent with the aureola of all virtues, says to us in the words of St. Paul, but with deeper significance than even he could give them: "Be ye followers of me, as I am of Christ."[1] Indeed we are drawn to follow Mary by the charm of a Mother's love and by the exquisite harmony of her gentle virtues, a

---

[1] 1 Cor 4: 16; 11: 1.

music which subdues and ravishes the soul far better than did the triumphant strains of that other Mary, sister of Aaron, who led the choirs of the daughters of Israel.[1]

---

[1] *Sumpsit ergo Maria prophetissa, soror Aaron, tympanum in manu sua, egressaeque sunt omnes mulieres post eam cum tympanis et choris* (Ex 15: 20).

REGINA SANCTORUM OMNIUM.

Fiat inter Stellas   *Luna minores.*

Erit mons domûs Domini præparatus in vertice
montium. *Micheæ 4.*

THE SALVE REGINA

This beautiful prayer was probably composed in the 11th century by the holy Benedictine monk, Hermann Contractus, with the exception of the last line, *O clement, O loving, O sweet Virgin Mary,* which was subsequently added by St. Bernard.[1]

The hymn begins with a loving salutation: *Hail, holy Queen, Mother of mercy, our life, our sweetness and our hope.* This prelude is followed by the prayer itself, which is full of life and of ardent love.

I know not whether to call it an idyll or a drama, divided into three parts. First we hear the lament of the *beginners*, who bewail their sins in this vale of tears. Next, we listen to the voice of the *proficient*, who long only for unison with Christ, the blessed fruit of Mary's womb. Lastly, there is the exultant cry of the *perfect*, who are inebriated with the pure delights of Mary's love.[2]

---

[1] Benedict XIV, *De Festis B. Virginis*, ch. 13, *in fine.*

[2] In the language of ascetical writers *beginners* in the spiritual life are those who are engaged in purifying their souls from sin. The *proficient* are more advanced, and are occupied chiefly in the practice of virtue. The *perfect* are those who have made considerable progress in virtue and are aspiring

I. THE PRELUDE

We greet Mary, first of all, as our Queen. *Hail, Holy Queen.* This title is most appropriate to the Mother of God. The Gospel tells us that heaven is a kingdom. All saints who inherit that kingdom are kings, *quot vives, tot reges*, to use the words of St. Augustine. Nevertheless the Church in her liturgy gives the royal title to none save Jesus Christ and Mary His Mother, whom she sometimes calls Queen of Heaven, *Ave Regina caelorum*, and sometimes she greets her simply as Queen, *Salve Regina.* The reason is that in heaven dignity and degrees of glory are proportionate to sanctity; and therefore the Mother of God, because she is the holiest of all, is Queen of all, Queen of all the "kings" in Paradise.[1] All the subjects of Jesus Christ own Mary's sway. Her throne is the highest and most glorious after that of her Divine Son. Her power is less than that of God alone. Her queenly graciousness is such as to encourage

---

to the highest and rarest degree of divine love. Perhaps these three grades in the spiritual life are referred to in the words of the psalmist: "Decline from evil and do good, seek after peace and pursue it."—Ps 33:15.

[1] In the Litany of Loreto we invoke Mary as Queen of Angels, of Patriarchs, etc.

us daily to greet her without fear: *Hail, holy Queen*. We hasten to add, "Mother of mercy." If as Queen she has power to obtain all things for us—as a compassionate mother she desires to grant us all that we need. The one title brings her nearer to God, the other nearer to us. The one recalls to mind the power that draws down grace from heaven, the other the loving kindness which lavishes that grace on every side. *Hail, holy Queen, Mother of Mercy.*[1] Assuredly mercy is an attribute of God, but His justice is as infinite as His mercy. In Mary all is mercy, and we cannot even imagine in her the sternness of justice. "There is in her," says St. Bernard, "nothing austere, nothing terrible."[2] Therefore we can and should fear God, whom we have offended: we can and should fear the Son of God, who will be our Judge; but we should not, nay, we cannot fear Mary, who is only Mother of mercy. *Hail, holy Queen, Mother of mercy.*

---

[1] This phrase is a Hebraism equivalent to *merciful mother.* Cf. "steward" and "mammon of iniquity" for *unjust steward* and *ill-gotten wealth*. See the learned commentary on the Salve Regina in the work *De Maria Deipara Virgine* (Bk. 5, ch. 3), by St. Peter Canisius.

[2] St. Bernard, *Serm. in dom. Infra oct. Assumptionis B. V. M.*

Furthermore we daily venture to accost Mary as *our life, our sweetness and our hope.* In truth, Jesus Christ is our life,[1] but it was from Mary that He first received His human life. He is our inexhaustible sweetness, but it was Mary who brought us this sweetness, as the honeycomb yields the honey. Jesus Christ is our hope,[2] but Mary is the harbinger and pledge of our hope, for it accords well with the harmony of divine action that as our hopes began with the Mother of Jesus, so they should also be consummated in her and through her. Therefore sinners have recourse to Mary that they may be restored to the life of grace: the just find in her the sweetness of spiritual joy; and all receive from her new vigorous hope of eternal happiness. *Hail, our life, our sweetness and our hope.*

---

[1] "I am the way, the truth and the life." (Jn 14: 6).

[2] "The hope of all the ends of the earth and in the sea afar off." (Ps 64: 6).

II. THE PRAYER

1. The Prelude is followed by the Prayer itself, which begins with these words: *To thee do we cry, poor banished children of Eve; to thee do we send up our sighs, mourning and weeping in this vale of tears.* This is the lamentation of the *beginners,* the prodigal sons who, with Mary's aid, are returning to God. They acknowledge that they are exiles upon earth, banished from heaven and from God, for the first effort of souls that turn to God is to detach themselves from earthly things and to aspire after the things of heaven. They confess that earth is for them only a vale of tears, and that their only inheritance is sorrow, that dearly-cherished sorrow of penitents which is worth more than all the fleeting pleasures of the world. But these exiles know full well that they are not orphans, that they have a mother in Mary, aye, a better mother than Eve was, and that she can and will soothe their grief and comfort them in their exile. They say therefore to her with full confidence: *To thee do we cry, poor banished children of Eve; to thee do we send up our sighs, mourning and weeping in this vale of tears.*

2. Here begins this second part of the

Prayer: *Turn then, most gracious advocate, thine eyes of mercy toward us.* To understand these words aright, we must remember that Jesus and Mary are the two great instruments employed by the Almighty for the accomplishment of His merciful designs. They are in the order of grace what Adam and Eve were in the disorder of sin, insomuch as that, to use the emphatic words of St. Augustine, the very flesh of Jesus, which is the instrument used in the work of salvation, is the flesh of Mary.[1] Hence as Jesus Christ is our Advocate with the Father, so Mary is our advocate with Jesus Christ.[2] We beseech her to look upon us with pity, to the end that we may obtain a compassionate glance from Jesus also. *Turn then, most gracious advocate, thine eyes of mercy toward us.* Happy shall we be if we obtain this favour, for we know from the Gospel that one glance from Jesus could change and sanctify the souls of men.[3] We immediately add: *After this our exile, show unto us the blessed fruit of thy womb.* He

---

[1] *Liber de Assumptione B. M. Virginis*, attributed to St. Augustine.

[2] "The Son will hearken to His Mother, the Father will hear the Son."—St. Bernard, *Serm. de Nativitate B. Mariae Virg.*

[3] Mk 10: 21; Lk 22: 61; Jn 1: 42; 19: 26.

who has once begun to walk in the way of the Lord seeks only to possess Jesus Christ. As beginners in the spiritual life think only of the tears of penance and the joy of forgiveness, so the one aspiration of those who are advancing in the path of holiness is to possess Christ, "to be with Christ."[1] But Jesus is ours only through Mary and with Mary. She gave Him to us at Bethlehem, and hereafter in heaven we shall possess Jesus with His Mother. Here on earth she has given Him to us as the infant in her arms. There in heaven she will show Him to us in His glory for all eternity. "The Queen stood at Thy right hand."[2] *After this our exile, show to us the blessed fruit of thy womb, Jesus.*

3. Lastly, the lament of the penitent and the prayer of the proficient are followed by the cry of love and of triumph which concludes the *Salve Regina*. It still breathes the tenderness of St. Bernard after the lapse of seven hundred years during which it has daily been on the lips of all who love Mary. *O clement, O loving, O sweet Virgin Mary.* There are moments in which the soul is filled with such

---

[1] Phil 1: 23.

[2] Ps 44: 10.

THE VIRTUES OF MARY

an excess of emotion that it must find relief in words. Mysterious moments are these of self-revelation! In such a moment the holy monk of Clairvaux, as he listened to the *Salve Regina* while it was being sung in the cathedral of Spires—where the place on which he was standing is still pointed out—could not restrain the impetuosity of his love and it burst forth into these tender and impassioned words: *O clement, O loving, O sweet Virgin Mary.*[1] These words are a revelation of the soul of St. Bernard, who loved our Lady after God with all his heart. They also beautifully express the incomparable attractiveness of our Mother. She is *clement, loving,* and *sweet.* She allures men's hearts by her clemency, she enamours them of her kindness and ravishes them with her sweetness. Who can withstand her heavenly charm? She is clement to suppliants, compassionate towards those that weep, she inebriates those who love. She is gracious to the penitent, loving to the proficient, full of sweetness to the perfect. *O clement, O loving, O sweet Virgin Mary.* St. Bonaventure, whose mind and heart were full of these thoughts, was wont to call Mary "the

---

[1] Ratisbonne, *History of St. Bernard*, vol. 2, ch. 37.

ravisher of hearts." Who will grant to us that Mary may steal from us our heart also, our heart which was perhaps in time past the slave of sin and the world? Ah! let us deliver this poor heart from its slavery and give it to her who is worthy to be its Queen, to the clement, loving, sweet Virgin Mary.

St. Bonaventure, with child-like simplicity, added: "O ravisher of hearts, when wilt thou give me back my heart?"[1] Nay, rather, let us beg her to keep our heart for ever and ever, and let us renew this offering, poor as it is, day by day while we devoutly recite the *Salve Regina*.

---

[1] *Stimuli divini amoris*, part 3, ch. 19. [a work once attributed to St. Bonaventure. Editor's note.]

The Academy of the Immaculate Books

Obviously there is a need for good, solid devotional books on Marian Shrines and Saints outstanding in their love for the Blessed Mother and the Eucharistic Jesus. The Franciscans of the Immaculate are attempting to meet this need and flood the market with readable inspirational books at a reasonable cost.

Special rates are available with 25% to 50% discount depending on the number of books, plus postage. For ordering books and further information on rates to book stores, schools and parishes: *Academy of the Immaculate, P.O. Box 3003, New Bedford, MA 02741, Phone/FAX (888)90.MARIA [888.90.62742], E-mail academy@marymediatrix.com.* Quotations on bulk rates by the box, shipped directly from the printery, contact: *Franciscans of the Immaculate, P.O. Box 3003, New Bedford, MA 02741, (508)996-8274, E-mail: ffi@marymediatrix.com. Website: www.marymediatrix.com.*

THE ACADEMY OF THE IMMACULATE

The Academy of the Immaculate, founded in 1992, is inspired by and based on a project of St. Maximilian M. Kolbe (never realized by the Saint because of his death by martyrdom at the age of 47, August 14, 1941). Among its goals the Academy seeks to promote at every level the study of the Mystery of the Immaculate Conception and the universal maternal mediation of the Virgin Mother of God, and to sponsor publication and dissemination of the fruits of this research in every way possible.

The Academy of the Immaculate is a non-profit religious-charitable organization of the Roman Catholic Church, incorporated under the laws of the Commonwealth of Massachusetts, with its central office at Our Lady's Chapel, POB 3003, New Bedford, MA 02741-3003.